Praise for *Smart Leaders, Smarter Teams*

"This book reveals how leaders' mindsets and actions get in the way of success, and what to do about it. Roger Schwarz, a renowned leadership expert, offers a wealth of pioneering, practical insights for leading teams more effectively. The payoff is a new approach to making teams more—rather than less—than the sum of their parts."

—**Adam Grant,** professor, the Wharton School; author, *Give and Take*

"*Smart Leaders, Smarter Teams* is a transformational approach to team leadership. It shows how to eliminate the hub and spoke effect of 'one leader, multiple reports' and creates a self-managing team that makes decisions, takes action, and gets results. I highly recommend this book and this approach."

—**Jay Hennig,** president, Moog Space and Defense Group

"There is no voice I would trust more than Roger Schwarz on the subject of getting the best from your leadership team. *Smart Leaders, Smarter Teams* makes it abundantly clear that when leaders foster an environment of transparency and trust, they set the stage for success now and for the next time. This book is for any leadership team striving to up their game and consistently get better results."

—**Kathy Council,** vice president, SAS

"All too often teams fall short of their potential. With *Smart Leaders, Smarter Teams*, Roger Schwarz—whose brilliant ideas are central to my courses on leading effective teams at the Wharton School—shows leaders that by changing their mindset they can create powerful team performance, productive working relationships, and positive individual well-being, so that each builds on the other and creates an enduring cycle of success and satisfaction."

—**Stew Friedman,** Practice Professor of Management, the Wharton School

"Finally a book has come along that offers practical wisdom about how leaders can develop great teams. It offers insight not only in to *how* but also *why* teams don't function as their leaders desire. This is a roadmap for transition for any senior manager who is looking to improve the operating system of their own leadership style."

—**Barton Hill,** managing director, global head of marketing—securities and fund services, Citi

SMART LEADERS
LEADERS
SMARTER
TEAMS

How You and Your Team GET UNSTUCK to GET RESULTS

ROGER SCHWARZ

JB JOSSEY-BASS™

A Wiley Brand

Published by Jossey-Bass
A Wiley Imprint
One Montgomery Street, Suite 1200
San Francisco, CA 94104—www.josseybass.com

Jacket design by Adrian Morgan
Cover photograph © John Cumming/Getty (RP)

Jossey-Bass books and products are available through most bookstores. To contact
Jossey-Bass directly call our Customer Care Department within the U.S. at 800-956-7739,
outside the U.S. at 317-572-3986, or fax 317-572-4002.

Wiley also publishes its books in a variety of electronic formats and by print-on-demand.
Not all content that is available in standard print versions of this book may appear or be
packaged in all book formats. If you have purchased a version of this book that did not
include media that is referenced by or accompanies a standard print version, you may
request this media by visiting http://booksupport.wiley.com. For more information about
Wiley products, visit us www.wiley.com.

Library of Congress Cataloging-in-Publication Data
Schwarz, Roger M., 1956–
    Smart leaders, smarter teams : how you and your team get unstuck to get results /
Roger Schwarz. – First edition.
        pages cm
    Includes bibliographical references and index.
    ISBN 978-0-7879-8873-9 (cloth); ISBN 978-1-118-22165-5 (ebk);
ISBN 978-1-118-23542-3 (ebk); ISBN 978-1-118-26023-4 (ebk)
    1. Teams in the workplace.   2. Teams in the workplace – Management.
I. Title.
    HD66.S394 2013
    658.4'092–dc23

                                                    2012046247

Printed in the United States of America
FIRST EDITION
HB Printing   10 9 8 7 6 5 4 3

For Kathleen,
Noah, and Hannah

Contents

Who this book is for, what it is about, and why I wrote it.

Why does a group of smart leaders so often create a less-than-smart team? This chapter describes how the mindset leaders use can get them and their team stuck. It explains why adopting a mutual learning set of values and assumptions gets you and your team unstuck so that you get more done and achieve your goals.

When you and your team try to achieve your goals by unilaterally controlling the situation, you get the very results you've been trying to avoid. This chapter enables you to compare your own mindset and behaviors to those of a unilaterally controlling leader, so you can understand the mindset from which you are operating.

3 Getting Unstuck to Get Results: The Mutual Learning Approach 49

When you shift to a mutual learning mindset, you and your team operate from a more productive set of values and assumptions. These include being transparent, curious, accountable, and compassionate, and creating informed choice. This chapter demonstrates how that mindset generates common understanding that transforms decision making to produce better team performance, stronger team working relationships, and work that is satisfying and motivating.

4 Getting the Puzzle Pieces on the Table: Mutual Learning Behaviors 1–4 87

How you think is how you lead. This chapter provides detailed guidance on how to put the mutual learning mindset into action through four mutual learning behaviors: state views and ask genuine questions, share all relevant information, use specific examples and agree on what important words mean, and explain your reasoning and intent. See how these behaviors lead you and your team to higher quality decisions, shorter implementation time, and greater commitment and trust.

5 Putting the Puzzle Together: Mutual Learning Behaviors 5–8 109

Continuing from Chapter Four, this chapter provides detailed guidance on how to put the mutual learning mindset into action through four more mutual learning behaviors: focus on interests not positions, test assumptions and inferences, jointly design next steps, and discuss undiscussable issues.

6 Designing for Mutual Learning 143

How you design—or redesign—your team shapes whether your team gets the results you want or the results you're trying to avoid. See how to enhance your team structures, processes, and context to get more effective decision making, less unproductive conflict, and greater commitment.

7 Dealing With Common Team Challenges   177

Most teams face challenges that are easily addressed by using a mutual learning approach. This chapter describes how to apply the mutual learning mindset and behaviors to deal with these challenges, including keeping team meetings on track, speaking with one voice as a team, preventing end runs, and giving and receiving feedback.

8 Becoming a Smarter Leader   199

Have you decided to become a smarter leader through mutual learning? This chapter helps you take stock of what you want to achieve, develop an action plan for what you want to change and why, and prepare to talk with your team about your changes. Together these steps will help you engage your team to support your leadership change.

9 Becoming a Smarter Team   215

Your team has greater power to get better results when you and the team decide to change together. The stakes are higher, but so are the rewards. This chapter provides specific steps to help you and your team take stock of what the team wants to achieve, develop a team action plan for change, and plan for team conversations to begin the change. Together, these steps will help you create a team whose results exceed the sum of its parts.

Preface

This book is about how you and your leadership team can get better results. Drawing on my more than thirty years' experience as an organizational psychologist helping leadership teams get unstuck and make solid progress, it provides practical, use-it-now advice backed by solid research to answer two of the key questions for team development: *What do I do to make my team and myself more effective?* and also, *Why do I do it?* Knowing why as well as how lets you improvise on the spot like a chef rather than plodding through a recipe and hoping the dish comes out right.

It's not simple or easy—there's no magic wand or silver bullet, and I can't promise that in three or four weeks your team will be changed forever. On the other hand, no one else can really promise you that, either. Instead, I give you straightforward principles and show you how to apply them immediately to address your thorniest and most vexing challenges. If you apply these principles over time, you will find that you and your team not only get stuck far less often, you also achieve higher levels of performance, have better working relationships, and enjoy greater well-being.

Teams are complex systems. It's not enough to focus just on vision, just on creating the right structures or processes, just on communication, or just on changing team member behavior. All these elements are important for your team to get results, and all must fit together to sustain strong results.

It's tempting to woo support by sidling up as if to say, "You're fine, but you need to get your team to change." Realistically, that's unlikely; a team is a system, and you're part of yours. This book starts with the assumption that you're probably making some contribution to your team's ineffectiveness in ways you don't see. You're not alone: all the leaders I have worked with were in some way unaware of how they were unwittingly contributing to the problems that plagued their teams.

WHO THIS BOOK IS FOR

The approach I discuss here is useful anywhere and in all areas of life, and will benefit anyone who uses it. However, it's harder to apply when you're working alone rather than in a like-minded group and feels harder to use for managing up. So I'm primarily addressing you as the head of a leadership team, with authority over the way your team is designed and how it works together, as well as ultimate accountability for the results your team gets.

Beyond the specifics of your formal leadership title, this book is for you if

- You believe values are an important foundation for your leadership and your team.
- Your team seems to be stuck, not getting the results it needs.
- You're willing to consider—just consider—that you may be contributing to the problems that are frustrating you.
- You're willing to learn from and with your team and recognize that you don't need to have all the answers all the time.
- You recognize that increasing team effectiveness is not something achieved in a day, week, or even a month. It takes time and effort.

OVERVIEW OF THE BOOK

Chapter One goes into more depth on the problem: why leadership teams get stuck, and what makes it so hard to get unstuck. It briefly introduces two contrasting approaches to leadership, unilateral control and mutual learning. Chapter Two takes up unilateral control and explores it in more depth, and Chapter Three does the same with mutual learning.

Chapter Four explores the first four of the eight behaviors that turn out to be most closely associated with acting from the mutual learning mindset, showing how they work to improve problem solving and decision making in the team and what's involved in their implementation. Chapter Five does the same for the other four behaviors, which all promote better performance, stronger working relationships, and improved well-being.

Chapter Six tells how to design your team to be congruent with the mutual learning mindset and behaviors and get the best results. Chapter Seven describes how to address typical team challenges, and Chapter Eight discusses ways that you personally can begin the process of changing your own approach from unilateral control to mutual learning. Chapter Nine extends the discussion, describing how you and your team can begin to work on mutual learning.

BACKGROUND

Smart Leaders, Smarter Teams builds on my previous book, *The Skilled Facilitator* (1996, 2002) which continues as a best seller and standard reference in team facilitation. That book isn't a how-to-write-on-a-flipchart or how-to-conduct-a-meeting kind of resource; it has endured, I think, because it shows professionals how to help teams increase their short- and long-term effectiveness. *Smart Leaders, Smarter Teams* boils that theory and practical approach down so that CEOs and other heads of leadership teams can use it to smarten their game.

Roger Schwarz & Associates has implemented this approach at numerous organizations since the 1990s, when the people at a leading computer chip manufacturer asked us to teach their leaders how to take a facilitative approach to leading. These leaders realized that, to be effective, they needed many of the same skills that third-party facilitators used in their work. Although access to a skilled facilitator was a benefit, it was no substitute for a having a team that could—in every meeting—use its own skills to work together to greater effect. While we continue to work with leadership teams to help them get better results, we also find that working with internal OD professionals and facilitators helps those leaders expand the impact of the approach across their organizations.

My interest in teams began long before I started helping them. As a teenager in the 1970s I worked with several other teens to start a suicide and support telephone hotline for people in our age group. We made decisions by consensus and I was often the one person who wouldn't give his consent. It seemed no one understood the situation as well as I did, but I wasn't able to persuade them and lacked the authority to overrule them. Looking back, I realize I didn't understand the situation better than anyone else, nor did I understand a lot about how teams get the best results. But around that time I also served as a counselor for twelve-year-old boys. I applied the first advice I ever received about leadership and teams: "People support what they help create." Determined to have them take responsibility for themselves, I successfully helped them learn to manage their own group in less than eight weeks.

Several years later, while a doctoral student in the organizational psychology program at the University of Michigan, I started to work with executives from the IRS and their counterparts at the National Treasury Employees Union. The two organizations had recognized that their traditional adversarial relationship wasn't working, so they were seeking a better way to work together. Initially with my professor, I facilitated the process and consulted with both parties, establishing teams in each IRS service center to implement the program and model the labor-management collaborative approach. The work became a model for improving productivity and quality through collaborative efforts. For a decade from the mid-1980s to the mid-1990s, as a professor of public management and government at the University of North Carolina at Chapel Hill, I taught and consulted to leaders on how to manage organization change and conflict, and I worked with governing boards, elected and appointed, as well as leaders responsible for managing cities and counties. These were groups that had to get results while working in—literally and figuratively—a political environment.

Since forming Roger Schwarz & Associates in the 1990s, my colleagues and I have continued to work with leaders and their leadership teams in organizations around the world. In all of this work, the goal has been the same—to help teams get unstuck to get better results. The results are increased performance, stronger working relationships, and greater well-being. This book is a way to share what we've learned so you and your team can benefit from it. I hope it serves you well.

January 2013   Roger Schwarz
Chapel Hill, North Carolina

How Well Does Your Team Really Work?

Why is it that when smart leaders gather to function as a leadership team, so often the team gets stuck? Why is it that the team as a whole seems less smart than its individual members? Why can't the team generate strong results? Why doesn't its supposed teamwork pay off?

Does the paradox and frustration of smart leaders working as a less-smart team describe your own situation? Consider these questions:

- Do you doubt your team really pulls its collective weight?
- During your team meetings, do you ever wish you could be elsewhere, or that the faces at the table could be different?
- When your boss—an executive or your board—asks you what your team is accomplishing toward a strategic goal, do you sometimes think, "What can I say that's both true and upbeat?"
- Do you suspect some of your team members resent how much time they spend in your meetings? Do you feel like much of your team meeting time is wasted time?

If you've been speed-reading up to now, slow down for a minute to really think about these questions: How effective is the team you lead at reaching its most important objectives? How agile is your team at recognizing major challenges and deciding what to do about them? What results does your team achieve by working together that its members couldn't gain by working independently? How much does the team contribute to your own ability to make the best decisions possible? How accountable do other members of the team really feel to each other for what the team must accomplish? How much do team members enhance one another's work outside the team?

You and your team you may be getting along with business and each other, but I can all but guarantee you that you are all working from a premise that hugely limits your team's potential. You didn't create this problem, but it's holding all of you back. The cause? The idea, widely held almost as an article of faith, that *there is one leader in the room.*

"ONE LEADER IN THE ROOM"?

What makes me so sure the team you lead falls short of its potential? The answer has to do with *mindset:* the set of core values and assumptions from which individuals and groups operate. It is the way of seeing that shapes every thought, feeling, and behavior. In even moderately challenging situations, virtually all leaders tend to use what I call a *unilateral control mindset,* despite the negative results it generates. Research conducted by Chris Argyris and Don Schön in the 1970s found that under pressure, 98 percent of professionals used this approach.[1] Their study covered six thousand individuals, and over the decades since then, my colleagues and I have analyzed thousands more cases in which our clients have faced challenging situations where they were not as effective as they wanted to be. The clients include professional men and women ranging from CEOs to first-level supervisors, including engineers, physicians, sales and marketing experts, scientists, HR and OD consultants, finance experts, and educators in corporate, governmental, and nonprofit organizations from more than twelve countries. Among all those thousands, we have identified fewer than ten leaders who did not use the unilateral control approach when a serious challenge reduced their effectiveness. Despite all the developments in leadership over the last forty years, when it comes to challenging situations almost all leaders slip into the same mindset. They have reasons for doing so, but there are also good reasons (and ways) to change it.

Traditionally, when people think of the leader of an organization, division, or team, they think of the *person* who has the greatest authority, such as the CEO, president of the division, or team leader. And almost always, they think of that person as the sole leader of that unit. They assign many leadership responsibilities to that leader, the most obvious being that the leader has the right and corresponding duty to make the decisions for the team. This perception of a leader as the one leader in the room translates into considering that leader solely responsible for all the leadership of the team: guiding the direction of the meeting, challenging the entire group's thinking, and raising concerns about team members' performance. This one-leader-in-the-room approach requires the one in the hot seat to be all-seeing, all-knowing, and all-doing, and to guide the whole content and process of the meeting. It's as if the team is a boat with one person serving as designer, captain, navigator, and engineer at the same time, and the rest of the crew merely show up and row.

Does any of that resonate with you right now? If so, it's no surprise. All leaders have run up against the untenable expectations and responsibilities of this traditional notion of what a leader does.

TAKE THE SHORT SURVEY

This book can help you with real problems you're experiencing as a leader on the job and in the other organizations that make up your life. To help you identify what's at the heart of the problem, go to www.schwarzassociates.com/resources/survey/. Complete the

(Continued)

survey—a three- to five-minute investment—and consider the analysis you see based on your answers. Each item gets at some aspect of how the unilateral control approach or mindset undercuts the actual effectiveness of a team. (The analysis is framed in terms of the core values of an alternative mindset called mutual learning that I introduce later in this chapter.)

STUCK IN UNILATERAL CONTROL: AN EXAMPLE

John Haley had recently been promoted to group president of a global design and manufacturing company. But John and his leadership team were stuck.

The business was underperforming financially, and they needed to turn it around. They were developing a new strategy but having trouble finalizing it and moving into action. In meetings, leadership team members would routinely agree to an element of the new strategy (or be silent) and then come to John individually after the meeting to tell him why he shouldn't follow through on what the team had apparently decided. Every time John held another team meeting to address the issue, people kept coming to him afterward with the same sort of advice. People weren't saying in the team what they were really thinking. Instead they were only speaking to John in private. This pattern made it impossible to get a real strategy in place to generate the numbers they needed.

Why were team members reluctant to discuss the issues in the full group? All the team members acted as though they were necessarily right and a win-lose atmosphere pervaded the room. If one member brought up an idea, others who disagreed would quickly shoot it down or dismiss it. People asked few questions of each other—and when they did, it was mostly to make a point, rather than to understand another member's view.

John needed his leaders to be more accountable to each other and to the business as a whole. Each of the team members led either a business unit or a staff function that supported all the business units. In John's mind, the team members were interdependent and needed to work closely together to identify and take advantage of potential synergies among the business units, but they weren't acting that way. To John, this meant that members needed to be asking each other about their businesses and challenging each other. But as John explained, "No one questioned the other leaders' business unit performance even though there was variability. No one said: 'Hey Joe, why are your expenses so high?' My fear was that they were doing it in their heads but not articulating their concerns."

Team members were reluctant to hold their peers accountable, partly because they were concerned about putting others on the spot and, in turn, being challenged by others. By going to John after the meetings, they thought they were being compassionate; they could raise their concerns with John privately and get them addressed indirectly, rather than having to air differences of opinion openly in the full group.

John wasn't aware that his own operating system—his mindset—was contributing to the problem he was complaining about. His unilateral control model of leadership led him to see it as solely his job to hold individual team members accountable, rather than placing a burden on them to hold each other accountable. This reinforced the team members' mindset that they didn't need to hold each other accountable. John and his leadership team were stuck; until they got unstuck, they weren't going to make any progress in turning the business around. John and his team needed a new operating system to learn how to get unstuck and to turn the business around. With time and work to change their mindset, they did just that. In a few months, they were able to craft a strategy that had the full support of the entire team and that they began to implement. The new strategy and the way the team worked together paid off. Over the next few years, the operating group increased their revenue by more than 400 percent.

WHY LEADERS STAY STUCK

I'm not the first to point out that leaders who use a unilateral control approach undermine the power of teams. Others have noted the inherent tension between acting from a mindset of unilateral control and simultaneously expecting that your direct reports share accountability for results.[2] So, given that the problem is widely recognized, why don't leaders choose another way? Why don't leaders simply get unstuck?

One reason is that, like John and his team, people aren't fully aware of the mindset they are actually in. In your own organization, I'm guessing you hear other leaders (perhaps your boss?) use language that espouses openness, cooperation, and the sharing of accountability between peer members of a team, but when you listen to or watch the same leaders in challenging situations, they seem to be guided by an opposite mindset, unilateral control, without recognizing the discrepancy.

This isn't simply a matter of saying one thing and doing another. If it were, it would be easy to change. The problem is that *in challenging situations, the mindset leaders use is rarely the one they think they are using.*[3]

For example, imagine that I gave you a situation with your team and asked you what principles you would use to guide your behavior—what I call your "espoused mindset."[4] Let's say you're working with your team to develop a strategy and you and the team members are at odds. In this situation, you might tell me that you believe it's important to get everyone aligned, important that all of them share their own thinking, important that others should try to understand different perspectives, for people to be curious, and so on. You might continue by saying that your role would be to create the kind of environment in which this discussion could occur. However, if I could video record the meeting and then dub in another face and voice in place of yours, you might well note that the leader's behavior doesn't seem to match the espoused mindset you shared with me. Instead of asking people what the group might be missing, the leader simply figures out what it's missing and tells others about it. Instead of trying to understand everyone's perspective, the leader tries to convince others why their view is wrong. It's not simply a matter of saying one thing but doing another. It's that the mindset that really guides the behavior is not the mindset you think you have. That sort of gap is easy to see in someone else, but human nature usually blinds people to it in themselves.

People tend to be unaware of using a unilateral control mindset. They use it automatically, without thinking about it. And that unawareness serves a purpose. It simplifies the problem and avoids an awkward realization of personal priorities: *What I really need to do in this meeting is make sure that no matter what happens, my solution prevails.*

When people *are* consciously aware of using a unilateral control mindset, they believe that what they're doing makes sense and that the behavior is for the good of the team and organization. From their own perspective, they are acting in a way that will get the best results, regardless of what others might think. Unfortunately, it won't.

A second reason leaders stay stuck, clinging to a unilateral control, one-leader-in-the-room approach, is the difficulty of imagining a workable alternative. Everyone knows that opening up decision making to the team can get the group stuck because people have conflicting ideas and conflict is inevitable, uncomfortable, and painful to deal with.

Team members don't want painful conflict either, so they help the leader stay stuck. They depend on the formal leader's use of control, reinforcing it even as they complain about it. They see it as the formal leader's role to raise and resolve difficult issues that are hindering the team's performance, even as they privately express frustration that the leader either doesn't see the issues or doesn't address them properly. They see it as the formal leader's role to give feedback to problematic peers even as they complain to others about not seeing changes in peers' behavior. They believe the leader ought to have personal insight into the leader's own contributions to team problems—while they withhold the information that would make the leader's understanding possible.

Leaders and members all think, "That's the formal leader's job. That is what leaders get paid for." Members expect the boss to make things happen without realizing that they themselves have a lock on the information on which action could be taken and need to be accountable for sharing that information, speaking up, and expressing their needs. As a result, all participants continue to act in ways that reinforce the roles and results they're dissatisfied with.

These aren't problems of being poor bosses or poor direct reports. These are problems with how people think of the relationship between a formal leader and team members. But when they do seek some other means of team success, they try sundry tools or programs that don't actually address or fundamentally challenge how they view the relationship between a formal leader and team members. They try "the participative leader," leader-generated "cultures of commitment," and the "empowering leader." They fill their leadership bags with tools to "motivate, inspire, and engage" others. But at the end of the day, they often feel weighed down by the tools and not much more effective as leaders. They seem like salespeople trying to get the team's buy-in to get things done. But all these methods allow everyone to cling to the same basic limiting assumption: that others need to change so that the formal leader's ideas can thrive, largely intact. Yes, the formal leader may need to make some superficial changes to help the team make major changes, but it's still the job of the formal leader to know what the team needs to do and how it needs to do it.

So that is how groups get stuck in a mindset of unilateral control. But there's good news: people can identify and change that basic limiting assumption. An alternative mindset to unilateral control and one-leader-in-the-room is available, and you are capable of achieving it.

CHANGING AN UNPRODUCTIVE MINDSET

You have a choice. You can challenge your team's mindset of unilateral control. You can ask yourself how true it really is that only others need to change. You can choose to accept the possibility that your ideas may not always be right. You can choose to put the team to work—a team whose members are accountable not just to you but to the team as a whole. You can choose to develop a team where all team members share in responsibility for the team's leadership needs.

Changing how you lead begins with changing your own mindset. Changing your mindset as a leader and changing the mindsets of other members of your team mean changing some basic assumptions and values you hold about what formal leaders do and how they interact with their teams, as well as your own role as the leader and your direct reports' roles as members of your team. Broadly, you will need to do four things to make this happen:

- Take on some fresh assumptions:
  - Leader work comes from every chair.
  - Team members also need to change.
  - Team members share accountability among themselves.
  - The whole team works from the same guiding ideas.
- Align structures (systems, policies, and processes) to support those new assumptions.
- Take an approach you can openly share and spread to others on your team and throughout your organization.
- Build trust across relationships.

Adopting Fresh Assumptions

The new assumptions I just listed will allow you to move away from a mindset of unilateral control. Here's how they each work.

Leader Work Comes from Every Chair

The reason leaders balk at the idea of shared leadership is that they are desperately clinging to control. But an effective approach for leading teams requires letting go of the mindset of control that results in one leader as the all-powerful, all-responsible sole decision maker for the group. Formal leaders do still need to hold responsibility for how decisions will ultimately be made. But they also need to spread control around the team and redefine team leadership as the ability to share responsibility for the team's functioning. This means that team leaders need to recognize that at any given time, the insight and ability to move the team forward productively might come from anyone at the table. That requires a redefinition of what it means to be the formal leader of a team—the leader isn't the *only* leader anymore.

Team Members Also Need to Change

The next assumption involves how the team thinks of the leader's role and how each member works with the leader. If the leader stops with personal change, over time team members who stick with old assumptions will behave in ways that force the only-leader-in-the-room role back into play.

How will they do this? Team members will gradually and naturally exert pressure that makes it happen. In a framework of unilateral control, team members see it as the formal leader's role to raise and resolve difficult issues that are hindering team performance and to give feedback to problematic peers as they complain to others that they are not seeing any changes in their peers' behavior. Team members figure the leader should just know whatever is wrong with anyone's behavior (including the leader's own), so it's OK for them to withhold the information that would help the leader see these things.

Team members need to realize that they are part of a collective team mindset that defines the relationship between themselves and their formal leader. They also need to see that leadership issues are not solely the concern of the team's formal leader, and that team leadership can—in fact, must—come from everyone on the team. They need to see that the leadership *role* is fluid, flexible, adaptive, and shareable in real time. For example, all team members need to see that at any time they can voice an observation that the team is making some perilous untested assumption. Any team member can and should help the team identify the key interests that are in conflict as the team tries to solve a problem. Any team member can and should help the formal leader see what's happening if the leader requests team input but seems to have already made a decision. When a leadership team learns to do this, they can work together as a more effective system. They are greater than the sum of their parts.

Team Members Share Accountability Among Themselves

If the relationship between leaders and other members of the team changes so that leadership roles are more flexible, it follows that the relationship among team members will also need to change. In the traditional team, accountability flows in a hub-and-spoke configuration. Members occupy nodes isolated at the ends of spokes, primarily accountable to the formal leader at the hub or center of the team. The formal leader, responsible for the overall team, therefore bears the stress of each spoke and keeps its node accountable. This traditional hub-and-spoke configuration assigns team members little real accountability and little need to commit to one another.

A better pattern can strengthen accountability and commitment. In it team members become accountable to each other, not simply to the formal leader. Team issues that team members would normally not address at all or talk about only to the leader become issues for them to address *with* the team. This includes their concerns about the team not meeting deadlines and about how work quality differences among team members may be creating a negative impact on them and other team members. This type of approach requires letting all team members identify what their strengths are and what areas they are trying to develop, so that they can give each other feedback and support. At the heart of team accountability is the notion that one of the most basic kinds of accountability is to give and receive honest if difficult feedback with your coworkers—no matter what your position.

Making this choice means asking team members to take more accountability for their team relationships and to use the leader less as an intermediary, arbitrator, or buffer.

The Whole Team Works from the Same Guiding Ideas

With shared accountability for team leadership, the team also needs to share a clearly defined common purpose and set of values. Without these guides, the burden again shifts to the leader to continually monitor and ensure that individual team members are acting in support of the team as a whole.

When the entire team has a shared understanding of and commitment to a common purpose and values, then the purpose and values themselves become guides by which team members can each assess their own performances.[5] In effect, every team member can lead using the purpose and values as guides. They can also explain to the formal team leader and to other team members how their intent and actions contribute to achieving the purpose in line with the values.

Focusing on these leadership guides isn't a way to avoid important and challenging conversations between the team members and the leader. It's a way to ground—or should I say elevate—interactions so that they don't devolve into conflicts based simply on what someone wants, whoever that someone may be.

When you choose to make purpose and core values central to the team, not only do you increase team members' accountability, you also increase your own. Some leaders find this increased accountability difficult because they feel it narrows their options. Other leaders see it as a way to walk their talk.

Aligning Structures with Your Values

By *structures* I don't mean organizational structures—who reports to whom—but rather the relatively stable recurring events that make up systems, policies, and procedures (like reward systems, budgeting processes, and performance management policies and processes). An effective team needs team structures that support the team mindset and the desired results. The structures that exist in a team aren't random; they reflect the mindset that consciously or unconsciously prevails in the group. You can consciously design or redesign them to fit the assumptions and values that you want to drive your team's behaviors. If your organization has been led using a unilateral control approach, it's a good bet your team structures will also reflect and reinforce that pattern in ways that undermine attempts to do such things as spread accountability.

The typical 360-degree review provides one of my favorite examples. Does this sound familiar? Your boss and representatives from your peer group, direct reports, and customers complete a survey, rating you on a number of items. Sometimes they add written comments. The completed survey scores are aggregated so that you receive a separate average score on each item from your peers, direct reports, and customers. Because most people have only one boss, you're likely to see that individual score. However, all the other scores and comments are anonymous. That's because those who design 360-degree feedback believe anonymity will lead people to be more honest in their evaluations. Often they also believe that performance feedback is the sole responsibility of the formal leader.

Unfortunately, this system has unintended consequences. First, the anonymity prevents you from learning who gave you the various ratings and what led them to do so. As a result, you have no way to assess the validity of the data. Second, without specific examples, you can't learn exactly what people mean when they rate you with "2" on "provides clear direction" or on "responds to my concerns." Finally, because the feedback is anonymous, you can't easily get help improving your behavior from the people who made the comments. In essence, a system that is supposed to help improve performance is designed in a way that makes it difficult to do so! At a deeper level, this kind of performance feedback system undermines the idea that team members are accountable to each other.

Our teams are filled with structures, procedures, and systems that were designed from a unilateral control set of values and assumptions that hinder team transparency, accountability, and ultimately effectiveness. If you want an effective team, the team structures need to support different core values and assumptions.

Avoiding What You Can't Share

Many approaches to leadership and teams become less effective as knowledge about them spreads. I heard a great example once on a plane—I was sitting one row in front of a sales executive and one of his managers, whom he had just hired. The executive was giving his new manager a tutorial on how to succeed in the organization. In great detail, he described (loud enough for me to hear every word) how he got others in the organization to do what he wanted. After sharing his methods, the executive said to his new hire, "Of course, I would never use these techniques on you." Much as I would have loved to see the new hire's face at that point, I resisted peeking back over the seat.

The executive's advice to the new hire was self-limiting. As soon as he told someone his strategy for exerting influence, he reduced the chance that his strategy would work on that person. Notice that the executive accurately described his approach by saying that he wouldn't use it on his manager. Self-limiting strategies are used *on* others. In general, the more people who know the strategy, the less it works.

This is a common problem in teams and organizations. Another favorite example is the sandwich approach to giving negative feedback: slip it between slices of positive feedback at the beginning and end of the conversation. Somewhere in your career, you've probably learned this approach. You were probably told that the first positive feedback is designed to relax the person and make it easier for them to hear the negative feedback that follows. The second positive feedback is designed to make the person feel better after hearing the negative feedback and end on a positive note, so the person won't be angry with you.

But if you've been a knowing recipient—maybe *target* is a better word—of the sandwich approach, you see the sandwich coming as your boss starts to serve it to you. You may quickly discount the positive feedback bread knowing that its purpose is to deliver the meat. You may feel manipulated and annoyed, or just amused that your boss thinks the approach would work on you. In any case, the strategy doesn't work as intended. Yet, amazingly, organizations continue to teach people this approach without realizing that the more they teach it, the less it will work!

If you're going to create an effective team, then the approaches you use have to become stronger—not weaker—as more people use them. That means moving from techniques that you use *on* others to an approach that you use *with* others.

Building Trust Across Relationships

Here's a situation I often pose to my clients so they can discover how they think about sharing information and power. In Table 1.1, the right column is part of a conversation between Paula and Ted. The left column contains Paula's thoughts and feelings. As you read the case, ask yourself two questions:

- What do you think the reporting relationship is between Paula and Ted?
- How should Paula change what she says to Ted if she reports to Ted? If Ted reports to her? If they are peers?

Most leaders quickly recognize that Paula is withholding relevant information that Ted could use to improve his performance in the future. Then they automatically make an inference about the reporting relationship—whether Paula and Ted are peers, whether Paula reports to Ted, or vice versa. About equal numbers of leaders opt for each of the three possible choices. However, when I ask them,

Table 1.1. Looking Behind the Scenes

Paula's Thoughts and Feelings	The Conversation
I thought the presentation was a disaster and so did three others I spoke with.	*Paula:* How do you think your presentation to the directors went yesterday?
Do you really believe it went OK, or are you just trying to put a good face on it? *Nit-picky!* You couldn't answer some basic cost questions.	*Ted:* I think it went OK, although there were some rough spots. Some of the directors can really get nit-picky.
I don't understand why you didn't emphasize why we wanted to do the project. The directors won't approve a project like this if they can't get answers to some basic questions.	*Paula:* We've got some really important reasons for doing it. Do you think they will OK the project now, or do we need to give them more answers?
I don't want to wait while this project dies on the vine. Besides, my reputation is at stake here too.	*Ted:* I think we're in OK shape. A couple of them came up to me after the meeting and said they appreciated the presentation. I think we should just wait and see.
I hope the directors don't think I'm responsible for your not having the answers to those questions. Why didn't you use the information I gave you? I've got to get you to understand what you've done.	*Paula:* Maybe, but I think we might want to give the members some more information.

"How should Paula change what information she shares and withholds depending on her reporting relationship with Ted?" almost everyone recognizes that, logically, Paula should share all the information regardless of her reporting relationship with him.

Yet emotionally, that's not so easy. Almost everyone's mindset about power and relationships leads to behavior that differs with peers, subordinates, and superiors. You might be very straightforward when giving feedback to a direct report but beat around the bush when giving similar feedback to your boss. When you act differently across your working relationships others notice and wonder who you really are. At a very basic level people question your integrity.

To get unstuck and get results, you need an approach robust and flexible enough to use in all your work relationships—whether you are working with people who have more power and authority than you, the same amount, or less; whether they are in your group or division or not; and whether they are fellow employees, vendors, or customers.

This doesn't mean you say and do the same thing in every situation; using the same approach means you use the same core values and assumptions to guide what you say and in every situation. Using the same core values and assumptions means you are acting consistently and—if you choose good values and assumptions—developing integrity. People come to know you as the same person, regardless of the situation you're in. In this way you generate trust with others. To create this trust means changing your mindset about power and authority relationships with your team and others.

MINDSET IS KEY TO CHANGING HOW YOU LEAD

At the heart of this book is the idea that how you lead is determined by your core values and assumptions—your mindset: the way of seeing that shapes your thoughts, feelings, and behaviors. If you're getting stuck, if you've changed certain ways you *behave* but aren't getting the kinds of results you want, it's because it's simply not enough to change how you behave. Your *mindset* leads to those behaviors and ultimately, those results. If you want to change the results, you need to change the mindset that causes you to behave the way you do.

This means moving beyond techniques. You've probably gotten advice many times to try a new technique to get better results. But

If you want to change the results, you need to change the mindset that causes you to behave the way you do.

this book isn't about simply trying new techniques, and I'm not making a quick-fix promise. If a simple change in technique could get you better results overnight, you'd already be using it. Simply learning new techniques or changing behavior without changing your mindset is likely to lead to more of the same problems you're encountering now. That's why many leaders become so cynical—often deservedly so—about leadership change efforts. If you have seen more than a few of these efforts come and go, you may view any new effort as the flavor of the month. Whatever enthusiasm you might have for a new approach to improve your leadership and the leadership of your team, it may be tempered by the belief that any change will be short-lived and will soon take its place alongside other efforts that were once touted and now collect dust on bookshelves throughout your organization. With each discarded effort, cynicism grows and sustainable improvement becomes more elusive. That's because efforts that focus only on changing your skill set simply don't have the power to create and sustain stronger results. For this, you and your team also need to change your mindset.

Changing your mindset isn't easy and it doesn't happen overnight. It doesn't happen by sitting through or even actively participating in a two-day seminar or a team off-site, or by just reading a book (including this one—sorry). If you need significant change to create sustainably better results, you need to make significant efforts commensurate with that deep level of change. That means working with your team, over an extended period of time, so that the team mindset takes a new form.

The choice here is between continuing to make changes only in behavior or structure while hoping for significant improvements or to begin to change your mindset and the mindset of your team that generate the behavior and structures. When you choose the latter, you choose to work on root causes. By understanding your mindset, you'll start to understand why you and your team are getting stuck, how you are unintentionally contributing to staying stuck, and how to get unstuck.

Your Mindset as an Operating System

Here's a useful analogy. Your mindset is like your computer's operating system. Every computer needs one to run. Without an operating system any computer is an expensive paperweight. A computer operating system organizes and controls all the computer's hardware and software so that the computer acts in a flexible but predictable way.

Your mindset does the same thing. You use your mindset to act and get results. Your mindset controls the decisions you make, the statements you make, and the questions you ask. Like any good operating system, your mindset enables you to take action quickly, effortlessly, and skillfully. It does this by using your core values and assumptions to design your behavior. It uses principles such as, "When I am in situation X and Y happens, I should say or do Z." For example, "If I'm in a problem-solving meeting with my direct reports and they are proposing a solution that I think won't work, I should tell them why their idea is flawed."

Like any computer operating system—Windows, for instance, or Linux—your mindset works very quickly so you can assess the situation and make split-second decisions that seem effortless. It's your mindset that enables you to immediately act and react without having to take time to think about it.

Just as you rarely think about your computer's operating system—unless there's a problem—you are also usually unaware of your own mindset. It works in the background so it doesn't distract you from the issues you are trying to resolve. When you're responding to your direct reports about the flaws in their proposed solution, you're not aware that you may be thinking, *These folks don't really get it. They don't fully understand the challenge here. I need to show them.* You just respond, seemingly without thinking. The fact that mindset operates without conscious awareness is a good thing—until it becomes the cause of problems.

To continue the computer analogy, if your mindset is like an operating system, then your behavior is like application software. Application software helps you accomplish a specific task. Think of the different applications you run on your computer, for example, Microsoft Office, Google Maps, or iTunes. In general such task-oriented programs are designed to be run with the background help of the computer's operating system and cannot run without it. The efficiency here is that the one operating system serves many house-keeping needs that all your applications share.

But this arrangement poses limitations as well, including the fact that the version of operating system you're running affects how well your application software runs. You know this if you've ever tried to run a new program, like a video game, only to discover that your operating system won't support it. If you're trying to run the most current versions of Google Earth, iTunes, or your favorite video game and you're using the current version of your operating system, your application will probably run happily. But try to run a 2012 program on an out-of-date operating system like Windows 95 and you'll be out of luck.

It's the same with people's mindsets and behaviors. Sometimes you want to change your behavior to get better results. You get excited by something you learn or experience, maybe even in a leadership or team development program. You hope you can install the program and run it like new software, and that you and your team will be able to accomplish more, better and faster.

Unfortunately, most of the time it doesn't work. Just as you can't successfully run a new computer application without a compatible operating system, you can't successfully implement a new set of behaviors without also changing the mindset that makes it run.

Organizations are littered with the carcasses of once-touted change efforts that focused on changing only behaviors. Look around your organization—check your bookshelf—and you may see some of these unfortunate remains. The sad part is that those behavior changes you tried to make could have been useful if they'd only had deeper support.

If a new computer application doesn't run well on your old operating system, you can simply upgrade to the latest version. But what if you're trying to implement new leadership behaviors and aren't getting better results? Where and how do you upgrade to the new mindset that the new behaviors require? You need to trade in the unilateral control mindset for one called *mutual learning*.[6] I introduce them briefly here, and go into more detail in the next two chapters.

The Limiting Mindset: Unilateral Control

When you use a unilateral control mindset, you are trying to achieve your goals by controlling the whole situation. This means trying to get others to do what you want them to do while keeping yourself minimally influenced by others. You view leadership as *power over* others, so it's important to hold on to it. With a unilateral control mindset, you think if you were to share power with others, you'd lose power. And that would be a bad thing.

When you use a unilateral control mindset and you're working with people who see things differently from the way you do, the essence of your mindset is simple: *I understand the situation, you don't; I'm right, you're wrong; I will win.*

When you use a unilateral control mindset and you're working with people who see things differently from the way you do, the essence of your mindset is simple: I understand the situation, you don't; I'm right, you're wrong; I will win.

Unilateral control leads to unilateral leadership. Sometimes it's blatant, but often it's subtle. You think of yourself as the sole leader in your team and that makes your team members followers. Consequently, you alone become responsible and accountable for the team's leadership. This means you guide discussion, challenge team members' thinking, and deal with issues that arise in the team and between team members. When members of your team have different points of view, you see yourself as the person who has the information, experience, and expertise to figure out what the team needs to do.

Continuing with the computer analogy, 98 percent of leaders have the unilateral control mindset preinstalled. For almost everyone around the world, it's the default operating system when faced with challenging situations. When the stakes are high, when you feel strongly about the situation or solution, or when others have very different views from yours—chances are you automatically run on this mindset.

The Transforming Mindset: Mutual Learning

When you use a mutual learning mindset, you achieve your goals by learning from and with others. This means you're open to being influenced by others at the same time you seek to influence others. You see each member of your team having a piece of the puzzle. Your job, along with the other team members, is to jointly put the puzzle together. You view leadership as power *with others*, not *over others*, so you look for ways of sharing it. With a mutual learning mindset, power is not zero-sum. If you share power with others, you don't lose any yourself.

When you operate from the mutual learning mindset and you're working with people who see things differently from the way you do, the essence of your mindset is simple: *I understand some things. So do you. Let's learn and move forward together.*

Mutual learning supports shared leadership. This doesn't mean that you give up your role as the formal leader of the team. And it doesn't mean that the team starts making all decisions by consensus. It does mean each team member is responsible for helping lead the team—taking initiative and sharing accountability for the team's functioning and results. It means that at any time, any leader on the team can express a key idea, take the lead in guiding discussion, challenge other team members' thinking, or help the team move forward in other ways. When members of your team have different points of view, everyone on the team becomes curious about what information each of you has to support your different views and what each of you might be missing.

When you operate from the mutual learning mindset and you're working with people who see things differently from the way you do, the essence of your mindset is simple: I understand some things. So do you. Let's learn and move forward together.

MIND THE GAP

It's easy to think you're using a mutual learning mindset when you're really using a unilateral control mindset. Mutual learning is often what forward-thinking leaders and organizations espouse and their fond beliefs are often touted in the press. Read the *New York Times* Sunday business column "Corner Office," which interviews CEOs each week about their leadership approach. Most of the CEOs describe how they create a safe environment for people to take risks and build trust, an environment in which people can be curious and learn from each other at the same time they create teams that are accountable. How congruent are these CEOs' behaviors with the mutual-sounding leadership approach they espouse? My hunch is not as much as they think. In my decades of working with leaders, observing thousands of behaviors, I've found that nearly all leaders who espouse mutual learning seem in fact to be operating from a unilateral control mindset. As a result, they undermine the very results they are trying to create.

Creating an effective leadership team starts with making some fundamental choices about how you want to lead. These choices reflect your basic values and assumptions about what it means to be a leader and what it means to be a team. I frame them as choices between a traditional but self-limiting approach to leadership and a relatively new, more systemic and sustainable approach to leadership. Creating this new approach to leadership and teams requires making a series of decisions. You may not have thought about your power of choice or, if you did, you may have assumed that the traditional approach was the only option. But you do have options, and the choices you can make about these leadership issues can benefit everything your team does. Ultimately, your choices govern the results your team can achieve. You can uncover and change your own mindset and that of your team—making yourself a smarter leader with an even smarter team.

CHAPTER

How You and Your Team Get Stuck
The Unilateral Control Approach

The mindset of unilateral control—which seems to come naturally to almost everyone in business—leads people to try to achieve goals by influencing others without being influenced in return. It defines leadership as *power over* others and makes sharing power with others feel like losing power—a bad thing, in that context.

When you apply a unilateral control mindset to working with people who see things differently from you, your essential perspective is a triple threat:

- *I understand the situation, you don't.*
- *I'm right, you're wrong.*
- *I will win.*

Consequently, you retain all responsibility and accountability when you're leading a team. You lead discussions, correct members' thinking, and arbitrate differences that arise between them. And when you're a team member, you expect the leader to do these things.

People tend to default to this mindset in moments of challenge. It determines how they walk when it matters even when their talk is something else. It's their background operating system.

WHY UNILATERAL CONTROL GETS RESULTS YOU'RE TRYING TO AVOID

A unilateral control mindset leads inevitably to unilateral control behavior, and the net effect is usually the opposite of what anyone wants. Instead of developing high-quality decisions that everyone is committed to, the team grinds out poor decisions that its members are reluctant to implement. Instead of improving working relationships and creating individual well-being, people trapped in unilateral control strain their relationships and create stress for themselves and others.

And when you get these unintended results, you're surprised. You certainly didn't set out to create poor decisions, resistance to change, defensiveness, and stress. Yet you have created, or rather contributed to, these outcomes. As systems thinkers like to say, systems are perfectly designed to get the results they get. The unilateral control operating system enables you to efficiently and skillfully reach ineffective results.

This moment of surprise is a gift—a heads-up to be curious and learn from the mistake. Unfortunately, few people embrace this gift and get curious enough to unwrap it. Most simply blame others for what went wrong. And those who avoid that pitfall tend to assume it was simply their actions that created the problem and so try to change what they do. For example, thinking your direct reports became quiet and defensive because you were simply telling them what *you* thought, at the next meeting you ask them plenty of questions and play down your own views. However, shifting from telling others your views to asking for their views is simply substituting one ineffective strategy for another—the people around the table will generally see your shift as a ploy, and will either keep quiet or attempt to figure out your view and play it back to you. Shifting only your behaviors or strategies simply gets the same ineffective results as before, albeit through different means. In short, your efforts to change your behavior lead you to unknowingly reinforce your unilateral control mindset.

Your *behaviors* aren't the root cause of your unintended results. The root cause is your mindset. As long as you are using a unilateral control mindset, you won't be able to consistently create the kinds of long-term results you want. Your underlying values and assumptions—sketched in Figure 2.1—will trip you up over and over again.

Values Built Into the Unilateral Control Mindset

Values are simply end-states their holders think worth striving for. A mindset, in its guise as human operating system, uses values as criteria for judgment and action. Using a unilateral control mindset means mixing these values to differing degrees and unconsciously designing your behavior based on them:[1]

- Win, don't lose.
- Be right.
- Minimize expression of negative feelings.
- Act rational.

Value 1: *Win, don't lose.* Having goals is essential to being effective as an individual, team, and organization. But in the unilateral control mindset, you value achieving *your* goals as *you* define them. Achieving your goals as you define them becomes an end in itself. You find yourself seeking to win, to come out ahead of peers or others on your team. You frame the situation as a contest in which there are winners and losers and you value only winning. When you observe or listen to others, you privately assess whether they're helping you achieve your goal or hindering you.

You consider things that others say or do that don't support your view as getting in your way. You consider it a sign of weakness either

Mindset

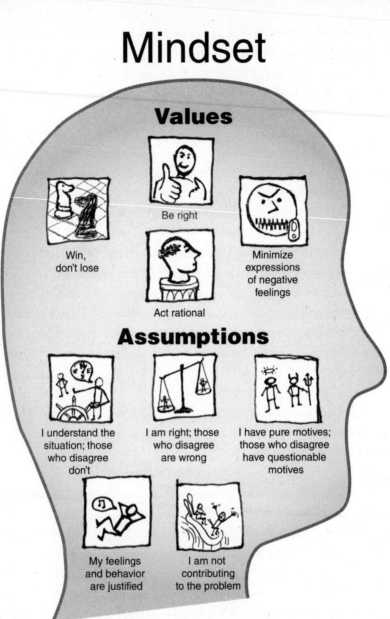

Figure 2.1. Core Values and Assumptions of the Unilateral Control Mindset

Source: Roger Schwarz & Associates; used with permission.

to change your goals or to achieve them in any other form than the way you originally envisaged them.

Value 2: *Be right.* Being right is a corollary of *win, don't lose.* When you value being right, you take pride in showing others that your views are accurate. If you have ever taken satisfaction in thinking or saying to someone, "I told you so" or "I knew this would happen," you know what it feels like to value being right.

Value 3: *Minimize expression of negative feelings.* Minimizing expression of negative feelings means keeping unpleasant feelings—yours and everyone else's—out of the conversation. This value stems from a belief that expressing anger or frustration or the like—or allowing others to express them—are incompetent behaviors. Expressing negative feelings may be seen as a sign of weakness or may hurt someone's feelings, both of which may make it difficult for you to accomplish your goals. In short, you believe that little good can come of people airing their feelings on a topic; it only leads to tension, wounded sensibilities, and strained working relationships.

Value 4: *Act rational.* The more you value acting rational, the more you expect yourself and others to remain purely analytical and logical. You believe that if you simply lay out the facts, all reasonable people will agree with you. You try to present issues as being purely objective, regardless of how you or others are feeling about them. You regard feelings as a barrier to good problem solving and decision making, instead of another source of important information. And the more you value acting rational, the more you want to be seen as having thoroughly thought through the matter at hand. When you discover gaps in your thinking, you try to prevent others from recognizing those gaps.

Assumptions Built Into the Unilateral Control Mindset

Maintaining the mindset of unilateral control also means making the following assumptions:[2]

- I understand the situation; those who disagree don't.
- I am right; those who disagree are wrong.
- My motives are pure; those who disagree have questionable motives.
- My feelings and behaviors are justified.
- I am not contributing to the problem.

Assumption 1: *I understand the situation; those who disagree don't.* This is the assumption that whatever information and understanding you bring to the situation are accurate and complete, and so are the conclusions you draw from them. In other words, the way you see things is the way things really are. If your team members hold different views, they just don't get it, are confused, misinformed, or simply clueless. If they understood what you understand, they would agree with you.

> *If your team members hold different views, they just don't get it, are confused, misinformed, or simply clueless. If they understood what you understand, they would agree with you.*

Assumption 2: *I am right; those who disagree are wrong.* This assumption is an extension of the first one. Here you assume that situations come with right and wrong answers and that your answer is, of course, the right one. People who disagree with you or see it differently are simply wrong. When you hold this assumption, you and the people with whom you are disagreeing cannot possibly all be right.

Assumption 3: *My motives are pure; those who disagree have questionable motives.* You consider yourself an earnest seeker of truth, acting in the best interests of the team or organization. At the same time, you question the motives of those who disagree with you. You assume they may be motivated by self-interest or some other inappropriate concern. Maybe they are trying to increase their power, control more resources, or even undermine your efforts.

Assumption 4: *My feelings and behaviors are justified.* Because others don't understand the situation as it really is (read: as you see it), because others are wrong, and because others may have questionable motives, you consider your feelings and behaviors justified. If you are annoyed or angry, if you need to end-run someone to accomplish a goal, or if you summarily pull someone off a project, it's all justified. Although you might have preferred not to do these things, others' behaviors left you no choice.

Assumption 5: *I am not contributing to the problem.* In the unilateral control mindset, you see your feelings and the behaviors that result from them as the natural and inevitable results of others' actions toward you. You don't consider the possibility that you're contributing to the very problem you're privately (and maybe publicly) complaining about. It doesn't occur to you that your thoughts and feelings may lead you to act ineffectively. In your view, all interactions go like this: others do things that are ineffective and you respond to their mistakes accordingly and appropriately. As a result, you see others as needing to change, not you. The only sense in which you may see yourself needing to change is that you may need to develop new ways to get others to change their ineffective behaviors.

> *You don't consider the possibility that you're contributing to the very problem you're privately (and maybe publicly) complaining about.*

RECOGNIZING THE UNILATERAL CONTROL MINDSET IN YOURSELF

Do you see any of this mindset (its values and assumptions) in your team members? Most likely you do. But how about in yourself? It's much harder to recognize when you're the one using a unilateral control mindset because your mindset usually functions in the background, out of your awareness. This works both ways; just as you can see it in play in others, those you work with can see it clearly in you. To change it, however, you need to be able to see it in yourself.

WHAT YOU CAN DO

If you want to know if you sometimes use a unilateral control mindset, answer the following questions yourself:

- When my team members have a view different from mine, do I think that they simply don't understand the situation and I do?
- When my team is having difficulty getting something accomplished, do I think that I'm not contributing to the problem?
- When I am working with my team, do I try to get them to buy in to my proposed solution more than understand their proposed solutions?

Then, if you have a coach or a trusted adviser who has watched you work with your team, test your answers by asking for some feedback on your leadership and explaining what leads you to ask. Present the same three questions about you, and ask for specific examples to illustrate the answers. Keep in mind that if your adviser doesn't have any examples for you, it doesn't necessarily mean that you don't use a unilateral control mindset. It might mean that your adviser is also operating from unilateral control and is trying to minimize the expression of negative feelings and avoiding a difficult topic with you—or may simply be blind to your unilateral control approach.

Ideally, you would have this conversation with your team. They know best how you work with them, and it's your team leadership you want to improve. But at this point, you may not have the mindset or skill set to have this conversation productively. If you are acting from a unilateral control mindset and team members tell you that, you can easily get defensive and shut down the conversation or respond in some other way that creates additional problems. This will be an important conversation to have with your team at some later point. If, however, you want to have the conversation now, ask a skilled facilitator—ideally one who uses a mutual learning approach—to help you have it with the team.

Unilateral Control Behavior

You use your mindset—your core values and assumptions—to design your behavior, which play out as you talk to others, send e-mail, and make decisions. When you approach a meeting assuming that you understand and are right and that those who disagree with you don't understand and are wrong, you think you need to convince others. Figure 2.2 summarizes eight behaviors you use to do that. Here is a brief description of each behavior and its results:

1. *State my views without asking for others' views, or vice versa.* That is, you either present your views alone or conceal them while asking for those of others, but don't get both sets on the table at the same time. As a result, you and your team end up talking past each other and you don't reach genuine agreements.

2. *Withhold relevant information.* Because winning is paramount, you share the information that will advance your views and withhold information that won't. As a result, you and your team make decisions without relevant information you should have considered.

3. *Speak in general terms and don't agree on what important words mean.* When you make a general statement—say, "I need some

Behavior

Figure 2.2. Behaviors That Follow from the Unilateral Control Mindset

Source: Roger Schwarz & Associates; used with permission.

of you to step up"—your team doesn't know who you're talking about and what you mean by "step up." As a result, the team can't meet your needs.

4. *Keep my reasoning private; don't ask others about their reasoning.* You don't explain why you are saying what you're saying and asking what you're asking. Sharing your reasoning would make you vulnerable to people challenging your thinking, which could reduce the chance that your view will win. Asking others about their reasoning might surface information that is at odds with your views, and it always increases the chance that they will ask you to explain your views—both of which decrease the chance that you will win.

5. *Focus on positions, not interests.* By focusing on a particular solution instead of the underlying needs you are trying to address, you and your team get dug into your positions and fail to craft solutions that meet team members' needs and generate broad commitment.

6. *Act on untested assumptions and inferences as if they were true.* Because you assume that you understand the situation and are right, there's no need to test any assumptions or inferences you're making. As a result, you and your team make decisions based on faulty information.

7. *Control the conversation.* To ensure that you win, you make sure that the conversation moves in the direction you want it to move. You make sure that people talk about topics that you consider relevant and that further your point of view. When they don't, you find ways to bring them back on topic. As a result, you don't get all the relevant information on the table and lose commitment.

8. *Avoid, ease into, or save face on difficult issues.* Because you want to minimize the expression of negative feelings, you don't address issues that could make others or you uncomfortable. As a result, you and your team don't get to the root cause of the issues.

WHAT YOU CAN DO

Do you recognize any of the eight behaviors in your team members? How about in yourself?

Tell your team members that you would like some feedback on your behavior as a leader. You might say that you're interested in learning whether you are acting less effectively than you would like to and ask them to give you examples of when you have used any of the eight behaviors, at challenging moments but also in relatively "normal" situations. Again, keep in mind that if they don't have any examples for you, it doesn't necessarily mean that you don't use these behaviors. It might mean that they are also using unilateral control mindset and behaviors and are trying to minimize the expression of negative feelings and avoiding a difficult topic.

Results of Unilateral Control

Mindset leads to behaviors, and those behaviors produce results. Unfortunately, the results derived from the unilateral mindset and behaviors are the very ones most people want to avoid. Instead of a high-performing team, you get lackluster performance. Instead of improved working relationships, you get strained relationships. Instead of developing individual well-being, you create stress for yourself and others. Figure 2.3 summarizes these results.

Lackluster Team Performance

The main result leaders want is better team performance: higher-quality decisions, greater innovation, shorter implementation time, and reduced costs. That's why teams exist—to create results that individuals alone can't. This is what most leaders think about when they think about creating a high-performing team. But if you try to improve team performance using a unilateral control mindset, the result is disappointing.

Results

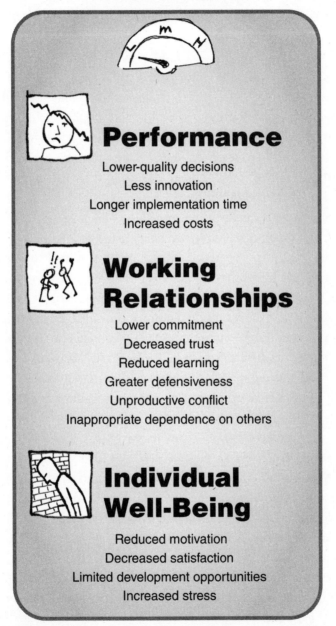

Performance

Lower-quality decisions
Less innovation
Longer implementation time
Increased costs

Working Relationships

Lower commitment
Decreased trust
Reduced learning
Greater defensiveness
Unproductive conflict
Inappropriate dependence on others

Individual Well-Being

Reduced motivation
Decreased satisfaction
Limited development opportunities
Increased stress

Figure 2.3. Results of Behaviors for a Unilateral Control Mindset
Source: Roger Schwarz & Associates; used with permission.

Lower-Quality Decisions and Less Innovation. Leadership teams don't make products or services—they make decisions. Some decisions are strategic; others are more operational. The better the decisions your team makes, the better your organization delivers its products and services.

To make high-quality decisions team members need to create a common pool of accurate information and a shared understanding of the situation they face. This includes understanding the different stakeholder needs that have to be met and crafting solutions that address these needs. But when team members are trying to convince each other that they are right and others are wrong, it's not surprising that the team will make poorer decisions than its members are capable of making on their own.

Innovation means creating something new, original, or creative. To create something innovative, teams need to become aware of and challenge the assumptions that have constrained their earlier decisions. But teams that operate from a unilateral control mindset have difficulty identifying—let alone challenging—their own assumptions. They can't think outside their own proverbial box. To identify and explore limiting assumptions, team members also need to trust each other. But when team members believe they are right and others are wrong, they often lack that trust and don't feel safe enough to raise the kind of unusual or even apparently crazy ideas that ultimately lead to innovations.

Longer Implementation Time. Teams often try to save time by shortening their time to make a decision. There's nothing wrong with that, but an effective team doesn't minimize just the time to make a decision; it minimizes the time needed to reach a decision *and* implement it. To focus on one without the other is like a pilot announcing to the passengers "We're lost, but we're making great time."

Systems thinking has a saying: "Go slow to go fast." Ineffective teams miss this key idea. Your team may make decisions very quickly only to learn later that it hasn't taken into account important information or addressed key needs. The team *increases* implementation time in several ways:

- Making decisions without the information needed to address key needs.
- Trying to decide and implement before clarifying things enough for individuals to fully understand the reasoning underlying the decision, so that they can do their part in implementing it.
- Encouraging or allowing team members to withhold information that needs to be understood during the planning phase, and then rewarding them for introducing it when it's too late, during implementation.
- Not ensuring team members' actual commitment and support before moving on from decision to implementation.

Sometimes your team may take a very long time to make decisions, or even be unable to make decisions at all. It may keep getting stuck at an impasse or stalemate, or it may find itself revisiting the same decisions again and again, as in the movie *Groundhog Day*. John Haley's team (described in Chapter 1) added Groundhog Day syndrome to its other troubles. By revisiting and revisiting decisions it had made about its new strategy, it delayed implementation and extended the time the business was underperforming.

Increased Costs. Poor decisions, reduced innovation, and longer implementation time often lead to increased costs. Poor and less innovative solutions can be more expensive because they fail to explore assumptions about what a solution does or doesn't need to do. Longer implementation time increases costs as your team spends extra time revisiting earlier agreements. One energy company found that because finance team members were not working closely with their internal project customers, their forecasts of capital needs was off by as much as 90 percent each month. This led to borrowing and paying interest on up to $450 million a month.

A global transportation company found it was carrying excess inventory costing $250 million a year. When I asked the vice president if this was a technical supply chain issue, he said no, it was simply a matter of his team not working together.

Strained Working Relationships

Effective leaders want productive relationships inside and outside their team. Effective teams improve the way they work together over time. But when team members operate generally from unilateral control, working relationships deteriorate over time instead. When your team doesn't have strong working relationships, then members try to minimize working as a team or collaborating with other members. They see the team as a hindrance to accomplishing their goals. They see team meetings as wasting their time, and so they disengage, figuring it's the leader's job to come up with any group-wide answers. Thus, unilateral control decreases commitment, strains working relationships, reduces team learning, and also promotes inappropriate dependence on others. Over time, you may lose some of your best talent. As the old saying goes, people take a job because of the organization and leave a job because of their boss—but it's probably their boss's mindset that does the damage.

Lower Commitment. You need your team's commitment to implement key decisions. But when you and other team members push their own solutions without incorporating others' concerns, team members whose organizational needs aren't met become less committed. Commitment also drops when team members believe they haven't been given all the relevant information. They say they will follow through on decisions, but they don't. When commitment drops, you're likely to find yourself monitoring team members to make sure they follow through on their responsibilities. That means that the burden of extra time and effort shifts to you. Over time, as the effects of decreased commitment add up, your team gets solutions that don't stick, and implementation time goes up.

Decreased Trust. When team members believe they are right and those who disagree with them are wrong and have questionable motives, they don't inspire trust in one another. When they withhold relevant information and keep their reasoning to themselves, they privately question each other's actions and motives, generating stories about how others aren't acting in the team's best interests. They see information as power to be shared with those they trust and withheld from those they don't, rather than a way to create common understanding and action. All of this tears the social fabric that gives the team strength.

Reduced Learning, Greater Defensiveness, and Unproductive Conflict. The faster your leadership team learns, the faster it can anticipate or respond to changing conditions, both outside and inside your organization. If your team isn't continually learning to work together to create better results, then the team and the organization are not getting a full return on its investment. Where unilateral control prevails, teams don't learn from their experience and find themselves rigidly repeating mistakes. Members simply seek to win and focus on their own positions. When they assume they understand and are right and that others who see things differently don't get it and are wrong, they have little interest in learning from others. Instead, they treat their own assumptions and inferences as facts, which adds to misunderstanding. Because they see their feelings and behaviors as justified and not contributing to the difficulty, they blame others for mistakes and defensiveness.

Simply put, members get into conflict when two or more of them pursue actions or solutions that are inconsistent with each other. Operating from a unilateral control mindset, they see conflict as something to win rather than as a puzzle to solve together. Teams that can't engage in productive conflict either avoid it, smooth it over, or end up in battles. If they address the conflict at all, they end up with stalemates, escalating conflict, or compromises in which everyone is dissatisfied—and losers disengage or seek to even the score.

You've probably seen what happens when there is unproductive conflict in your team. You need a meeting before the meeting to plan how to deal with team members you think will want to take the team in a different direction. Then you need a meeting after the meeting to make sure that they will keep their word or plan how to further influence or neutralize them if they haven't come around to your point of view. All of this effort does not resolve conflicts—and it weakens your team's ability to work together in the future.

Inappropriate Dependence on Others. In teams with healthy working relationships, team members appropriately depend on one another. Team members manage their working relationships directly with each other, rather than depending on the leader or anyone else to serve as intermediary.

A framework of unilateral control breeds inappropriate dependencies within the team, as members shift their burden onto others—including onto the leader. If Sean and Marla are on your team and Sean comes to you frustrated that Marla is not supporting his group, you might agree to talk to Marla for Sean instead of having Sean directly resolve the issue with Marla. If you do this, you contribute to unnecessary and inappropriate dependence on yourself and reduce Sean's accountability for his behavior.

If you find yourself spending too much of your time managing relationships for your team members, and not having enough time to meet your own goals, you're probably accepting the burden that others are trying to shift to you. As a result, you're likely to be frustrated with those members and with yourself. This further strains working relationships.

Less Individual Well-Being

The third area of results is individual well-being. In effective teams, team members—including the formal leader—find the overall team experience satisfying rather than frustrating. They find the work motivating, enjoy the work they do, and don't find it too stressful. In ineffective teams, unilateral control often leads to opposite results.

Although leaders worry when their team members don't seem motivated, some leaders shortsightedly think that the larger well-being of their team members is nice to have but not worth investing in. But if team members aren't feeling motivated or don't enjoy their work, and if they feel undue stress, that will ultimately undercut the team's working relationships and performance, creating more challenges for the team.

In the short run, most team members are more than willing to put aside their needs for well-being to help the team and organization achieve its goals. But over time, if they don't get these needs met, they feel stuck, anxious, overwhelmed, and taken advantage of. They feel they're giving significantly more than they're getting in return, so they disengage or become difficult to work with. Either behavior can reduce your team's ability to accomplish its goals and can strain team relationships.

Sometimes competent yet dissatisfied leaders leave the team or organization for reasons like these, which is not in the team's best interest. Executives in a computer chip company that dominates its market found this out the hard way. Many of its leaders had become wealthy through company stock; they could retire any time they wanted. They stayed because they liked the challenge and excitement of the work. But a number of these leaders told me that they were thinking of leaving and that others had already left. Even though the work itself was still motivating, the relationships with team members were difficult, and as a result their satisfaction was low and their stress was high. They didn't need the organization financially and they could create their own motivating work elsewhere. Fortunately, the organization realized that if many of these leaders left, it would suffer a debilitating brain drain, and it quickly made working relationships and well-being a top priority.

It's easy to dismiss this story, especially if none of your team members are wealthy enough to retire. But you'll find that increasingly people are willing to leave if their needs for well-being aren't met. In the past, people felt a stronger loyalty to their organization. This was partly a result of the social contract that organizations struck with them: work hard for us, be loyal to us, and we'll take care of you with secure employment. With that understanding, people were willing to sacrifice their well-being for long periods. That paradigm is all but gone. In recent years, employees at all levels have seen that social contract unravel. There are no guarantees—not even any promises. Leaders and those who work for them don't have the same level of loyalty and they're less willing to sacrifice their well-being. They're more willing to trade compensation for a work life that fits their individual needs and lifestyle. If you ignore this, you imperil your team.

HOW UNILATERAL CONTROL REINFORCES ITSELF

The insidious thing about the unilateral control mindset is that it reinforces the very results you and your team are trying so hard to avoid. When you use unilateral control, you generate lackluster results. As the arrows bordering Figure 2.4 suggest, the frustration you feel when you get these results reinforces your certainty that you understand the situation and others don't, that your feelings and unilateral behavior are justified, and that you're not contributing to the problem. If other team members would just do what you need them to do, the team would get the results it needs! Your mindset in turn reinforces your controlling behaviors; you believe that if you push harder, you will get better results. But pushing harder—or checking out in frustration—simply leads to more of the same poor results, again reinforcing your mindset. The harder you try, the less things improve.

At the same time, other team members are also likely to be frustrated with the team's results and, like you, use a unilateral control approach to try to improve the situation. Their mindsets and behaviors will also reinforce the unilateral control approach, so that the more everyone tries to turn things around, the worse things get.

Keep in mind that it doesn't take active malevolence to create this downward spiral. Almost all the time, when you and others are using a unilateral control approach, you all genuinely believe you're doing the right thing for the team.

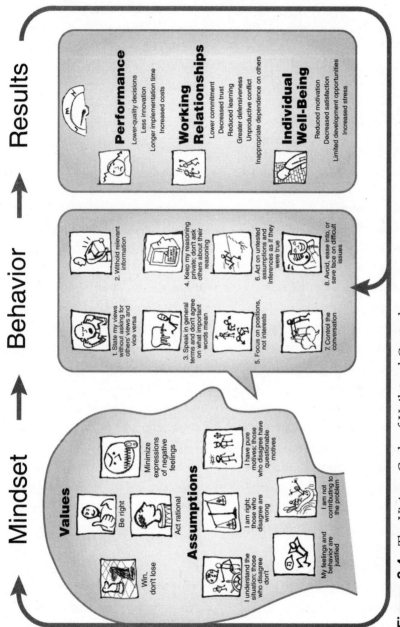

Mindset → Behavior → Results

Mindset

Values

Win, don't lose

Be right

Act rational

Minimize expressions of negative feelings

Assumptions

I understand the situation; those who disagree don't

I am right; those who disagree are wrong

I have pure motives; those who disagree have questionable motives

My feelings and behavior are justified

I am not contributing to the problem

Behavior

1. State my views without asking for others' views and vice versa

2. Withhold relevant information

3. Speak in general terms and don't agree on what important words mean

4. Keep my reasoning private; don't ask others about their reasoning

5. Focus on positions, not interests

6. Act on untested assumptions and inferences as if they were true

7. Control the conversation

8. Avoid, ease into, or save face on difficult issues

Results

Performance

Lower-quality decisions
Less innovation
Longer implementation time
Increased costs

Working Relationships

Lower commitment
Decreased trust
Reduced learning
Greater defensiveness
Unproductive conflict
Inappropriate dependence on others

Individual Well-Being

Reduced motivation
Decreased satisfaction
Limited development opportunities
Increased stress

Figure 2.4. The Vicious Cycle of Unilateral Control

Source: Roger Schwarz & Associates; used with permission.

Almost all the time, when you and others are using a unilateral control approach, you all genuinely believe you're doing the right thing for the team.

DO YOU HAVE A CHOICE?

How did leaders get to be unilaterally controlling? Is it possible to change?

Humans absorb the unilateral control mindset in a couple of ways. First, most of us are socialized to adopt it. Most of us went to schools that used a unilateral control approach and most of us had teachers that modeled unilateral behavior. Although we may have rebelled against it (I spent more than my share of time in the principal's office), by the time we graduated from high school we had adopted it ourselves. By the time we took our first jobs, we were skilled in ways to indirectly push our own views, withhold information when sharing it didn't serve our needs, and guide conversations so they avoided topics we didn't want to address.

We joined organizations that were built on unilateral control. Leadership and management research and practice began with trying to control behavior. That tradition continues today, but our culture uses more sophisticated language to hide it. When I ask clients, "Do you recognize the unilateral control approach in your organization?" almost everyone says, "I do." When I ask, "Do you recognize the unilateral control approach in your own behavior?" a large majority of them agree. Keep in mind, few people consciously set out to adopt this operating system that gets poor results, but we do it, and we learn how to apply it better—more consistently and enthusiastically— over time.

In addition, the human brain is built to use the unilateral control mindset in difficult situations. A simplified version of the biology is that when you face a potential threat, your brain receives and analyzes this input in two separate ways. One channel goes from your eyes and ears to your *amygdala*, a part of the brain that deals with fear and other emotional responses. The amygdala serves as an early warning detection system, enabling your body to prepare for whatever action you may need to take, such as run, fight, or hide. The other channel goes to your *neocortex*, the part of the brain responsible for higher-order reasoning. The neocortex enables you to analyze your feelings to determine whether and how you should respond. However, the route to the amygdala is quicker and the amygdala responds to the input before the neocortex gets a chance to intervene. That means that your emotional response kicks in literally before you have time to think about it.

You might wonder why the brain is designed so that we sometimes act before we can think. The answer, from an evolutionary perspective, is that it has helped us survive. When our distant ancestors encountered what could be a large threatening animate object, they were much more likely to survive if they could start running before having to figure out exactly what the potential foe was. This makes sense from a risk management perspective. If you run away from an apparent threat that turns out to be nothing, you're just out of breath. But if you fail to run away from a threat that's real, you may end up permanently out of breath. So you're programmed to err on the side of caution. Although few large, life-threatening objects inhabit the average office environment, the amygdala still responds to modern-day threatening stimuli as though physical survival were at stake.

To return to the computer analogy, you can say that we're dealing with out-of-date biological hardware (the amygdala) that sometimes creates problems for us, but we can't replace that hardware. (At least not yet, and I personally wouldn't want to be the guinea pig.) We need to change how we think with the hardware we have, and we can upgrade our operating system software by changing our mindset. That means becoming aware of the mindset you are presently in and logically assessing how suitable it is to the moment. Even though it's natural to use unilateral control in some situations, and most people have learned to overuse it, it's not inevitable that you use it, even at challenging times, once you realize there's a more effective choice.

CHAPTER 3

Getting Unstuck to Get Results

The Mutual Learning Approach

When you're operating from a unilateral control mindset, it can be hard to imagine any alternative. But very few leaders operate from unilateral control all the time. Most leaders also have—and sometimes use—another mindset that gets much better results. It's called *mutual learning*. With practice, people generally find they are capable of using it even in very challenging situations when they previously used unilateral control. In short, it is possible to design a team to support and embody the mutual learning mindset.

Figure 3.1 shows the core values and assumptions that constitute the mutual learning mindset. Contrast it with Figure 2.1—the set for unilateral control.

VALUES OF THE MUTUAL LEARNING MINDSET

Focus now on the five core values in Figure 3.1. The first two work as a complementary pair.

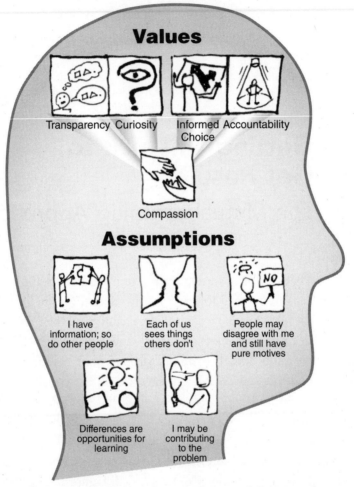

Figure 3.1. Core Values and Assumptions of the Mutual Learning Mindset

Source: Roger Schwarz & Associates; used with permission.

Transparency and Curiosity: Creating a Common Pool of Understanding for Better Results

Together, transparency and curiosity help you create a common pool of information and understanding between yourself and others. Everything you do as a mutual learning leader relies on combining the two. When you are transparent, others learn what you know, think, and feel. When you are curious, you learn what others know, think, and feel.

Transparency means sharing all relevant information—including your thoughts, feelings, and strategies—with the appropriate people at the appropriate time. It means explaining why you're saying what you're saying, why you're asking what you're asking, and why you're doing what you're doing.

If you think it doesn't make sense to start a project until next quarter, you say that and explain how you reached that conclusion—perhaps in these terms:

"I don't think it makes sense to start until next quarter. We won't have the key staff available before then and the market demand hasn't picked up yet. If we wait until next quarter, we can accomplish the project with the talent we need and still be ahead of the demand curve. Anyone see any problems if we wait until next quarter?"

If you're asking someone whether they sent out a report that was due yesterday, you explain why you want to know: "I'm asking because I need to get a copy to Jan by close of business today" or "I'm asking because I have some updated figures that I'd like to add if you haven't finished it yet."

Your explanation helps others understand what you are really asking. If you think a meeting is going off track and you want to bring it back on track, rather than just unilaterally switching the topic back to what you think it should be, you might say:

"It looks like we're trying to solve these operational issues. I don't see that as the purpose of this meeting. I'm thinking today we're just agreeing on what the issues are and who will own them. Anyone have a different view on that?"

You value transparency because you realize that other team members can't know what you're thinking and that knowing what each person is thinking is necessary to get all the information on the table and move forward together. This is true especially when team members differ.

It's difficult to be transparent when you're using a unilateral control mindset; you would have to share information that doesn't support your solutions, disclose why you really want to know what you're asking, and reveal that you are, in fact, trying to unilaterally control the situation. Sharing this information would undermine your approach and your ability to win. But being transparent when using a mutual learning mindset actually increases your effectiveness and enhances your strategy because your strategy is to learn jointly rather than control the situation.

When I talk with leaders about transparency, sometimes someone responds, "I'm transparent. I tell people exactly what I'm thinking." But transparency isn't simply telling people exactly what you're thinking. You have to be thinking in a form that's useful to share. At times, everyone has thoughts about coworkers that wouldn't be helpful to share in the terms that come to mind. Doing so isn't being transparent; it's a recipe for creating defensiveness in others and unproductive conflict.

A software company CEO routinely told his team members what he was thinking—that included telling them they weren't very smart and that they didn't know how to manage their parts of the business.

But transparency isn't simply telling people exactly what you're thinking. You have to be thinking in a form that's useful to share.

Team members learned not to disagree with the CEO and to avoid him if possible. Eventually several members left the team and organization because they found the environment so toxic.

Curiosity is the partner of transparency. When you're

transparent, you share information so others can learn about your thinking. When you're curious, you ask questions to learn about others' thinking.

If you realize that you have some of the pieces of the puzzle and that people you're working with have other pieces, you will be curious to know more. You will realize that much of what you think you know about others is just an educated guess at best; to really know, you need to ask them.

The mechanics of curiosity are simple: you ask questions that you don't already know the answers to. If you're wondering why your team members are pursuing an acquisition that doesn't seem to fit with the organization's strategy, you might simply ask them, "I don't see how this acquisition fits the criteria for our growth strategy and entering new markets. Can you explain to me how you see it fitting in?"

Developing a mindset of curiosity is more difficult than understanding the mechanics. In challenging situations, it's natural to believe that you understand and are right, while those who disagree don't understand and are wrong. Curiosity gives way to frustration as you wonder why others don't understand what is so obvious. So the questions that come to mind are uncurious, even belligerent, and designed to make a point: "You don't really believe that will work, do you?" or "What *were* you thinking about, if you were thinking?"

The Power of Transparency and Curiosity

Many researchers have found that transparent and curious leaders produce the three main benefits of the mutual learning approach: improved performance, better team relationships, and greater individual well-being. The endnotes throughout this section list the most relevant of these studies. Transparency, for example, offers these benefits:

- Teams that share more information with each other perform better.[1]

- When leaders are more transparent, followers are more accepting of difficult organizational changes, a key element in reducing implementation time.[2]

- When team members are more transparent with each other, they create a more collaborative culture and consider their team more effective.[3]

- In teams with significant power differences, the easier it is for team members with less power to speak up, the more success the team has in implementing new technology change.[4]

- Teams of physicians diagnosed patients more accurately when the team members explicitly shared their reasoning.[5]

- Teams that share more information among their members have less unproductive conflict.[6]

Transparency can even reduce the number and costs of legal settlements. In one study, a hospital found that when doctors promptly disclosed medical errors and offered earnest apologies, and hospitals offered fair compensation, the hospital's legal defense costs and the money it had to set aside to pay claims were each cut by two-thirds.[7] The time taken to dispose of cases was cut in half. In the thirty-seven cases in which the hospital acknowledged a preventable error and apologized, only one patient filed suit. It turns out that most patients who sue are responding not to the initial mistake but to the attempts to deny it.

Teams that share more information among their members also have greater trust, a key element in any team's success.

- Organizational researcher James O'Toole calls trust "the strongest glue binding people together in groups." Trust requires honesty and transparency. So it's not surprising that leadership researchers Kouzes and Posner found that in every survey they conducted, honesty was the top characteristic that managers sought from their bosses.[8]

- But leaders and team members can't create trust directly; it's an outcome of their behaviors and interactions.[9]

- Leaders who are more transparent instill higher levels of trust in their employees.[10]
- At the individual level, leader transparency is linked to higher employee motivation and job satisfaction.[11]

Regarding curiosity:

- Teams with a higher level of curiosity are more creative and perform better.[12]
- Managers who are more curious are more effective at solving complex problems. They find problem solving easier, seek more information about the problem, address more aspects of the problem with their solutions, and are more likely to avoid crises that stem from insufficient or excessive actions in responding to complex problems.[13]
- Curiosity is also an important contributor to generating work-place learning and better job performance.[14]
- People who are curious make better decisions after unforeseen changes in their work environment.[15]

People who are curious also interact more effectively with others:

- They tend to be less dogmatic in their ideas, more willing to consider different opinions, and more likely to consider the quality of the other person's reasoning.[16]
- They also tend to be more open to all kinds of situations, and less likely to deny conflicts than people who are less curious.[17]

In contrast, people who are less curious feel threatened when they learn new information that is inconsistent with their beliefs. They quickly shift from trusting to mistrusting others, and they engage in other forms of black-and-white thinking. All of this makes it difficult to manage complex and quickly changing situations.[18]

People who are curious:

- Have a higher tolerance for dealing with uncertainty.[19]
- Have an advantage detecting others' emotions and connecting with other people.[20]
- Are comfortable working through doubts and mixed emotions in relationships.[21] This is an advantage when negotiating emotionally challenging situations since they are able to remain open and engaged.[22]
- Perhaps not surprisingly, not only do they ask a lot of questions, they also reciprocate by sharing information about themselves.[23]
- Are more curious in negotiations about the other side's needs and interests and are more likely to get more gains for both parties.[24]
- And also have greater well-being. They report greater satisfaction and meaning in their lives.[25]

Combining Transparency and Curiosity

I talk about transparency and curiosity together because each requires the other. Research shows that in more effective teams, members move back and forth between being transparent and being curious, without getting stuck in just one of these modes.[26] By being simultaneously transparent and curious, you learn what others are thinking and they learn what you're thinking. This creates the common understanding you need to make decisions that generate commitment.

Informed Choice and Accountability: For Better Decisions and Commitment

The common pool of information you create through transparency and curiosity is necessary but not sufficient. You and those you work with need to transform that information into decisions that people can and will carry out. That's the role of informed choice and accountability.

Informed choice means making decisions (and maximizing others' ability to make decisions) based on the information generated through transparency and curiosity. When you value informed choice, you create situations in which decisions are based on pooled knowledge. Not only are you informed; so, too, are those you're working with. When your team makes informed choices they become more committed to the decisions.

Informed choice doesn't mean that everyone gets to make whatever decision they like or even that everyone gets to make the decision. The mutual learning approach doesn't change the formal leader's rights and obligations to make decisions. In mutual learning, the team leader maintains a full range of decision-making options, ranging from making the decision independently and without consulting with others to making decisions by consensus. However, in the mutual learning approach, you seek to maximize the informed choice for everyone. People tend to support the decisions they are able to influence.

When you operate from a unilateral control mindset, informed choice threatens your chances of winning: if people get to make informed choices, they may choose differently than you wanted. But when you operate from a mutual learning mindset, you see that maximizing informed choice for all increases the chances of a good decision, one the team will commit to.

You should be using informed choice long before you reach any final decisions on an issue. Throughout a meeting, conversation, or project, hundreds of little decisions are made: Who gets invited to which meeting? Who gets to see what information? Who gets to speak? Whose ideas are considered or ignored? If you value informed choice, you build it into those small decisions along the way.

Accountability is the partner of informed choice. When people make informed choices, they're also accountable for the choices they make. Leader accountability implies three expectations:

- You willingly accept the responsibilities inherent in your leadership position to serve the well-being of the organization.
- You expect that your name will be publicly linked to your actions, words, or reactions.

- You expect to be asked to explain your beliefs, decisions, commitments, or actions to your team and others.[27]

Accountability probably makes you think first of willingness to accept the responsibilities that come with your formal position. This includes being accountable for the short-term and long-term consequences of the decisions you make as part of your responsibilities. But notice that although you may be accountable to one or more people, the purpose of your accountability isn't ultimately to meet their needs, or even your team's needs, but to serve the well-being of the organization. This somewhat independent point of reference is critical for evaluating your actions.

Having your name publicly linked to your actions, words, or reactions means that people can easily know that what was said, done, or decided was what *you* said, did, or decided. This kind of accountability shows up in small but powerful ways. It's the difference between saying "It was decided" and "I decided." It's the difference between saying "Don't tell anyone I said this" and "If you talk to anyone about this, please let them know what I said."

Accountability also means that you're expected to explain your reasoning, decisions, and actions to others. It's not sufficient to simply tell others what you said, what you did, or what you decided. You have to explain what led you to say what you said, do what you did, or decide what you decided. By helping others understand your thinking, you reduce the chance that people will make up inaccurate stories about your intent.

Growing up, my sister had tacked on her bulletin board a quote from a poet (I've forgotten the source) that captured the essence of unilateral control: "To those who are important to us, we give explanations; to those who aren't important, we don't. And those who aren't important can tell the difference." In mutual learning, you owe an explanation not only to those who have more power and authority than you, but to all of those with whom you're interdependent.

When you operate from a unilateral control mindset you may try to hold team members accountable without making yourself accountable. Or you may not even dare to go that far because you don't want them to put *you* on the spot.

But when your mindset is mutual learning, not only do you want to hold others accountable, you want to be held accountable. You don't see accountability as a burden but rather as a way to honor commitments you've made that will help you and others achieve results.

The Power of Informed Choice and Accountability

The research shows that when leaders create informed choice and accountability, results are better for performance, working relationships, and individual well-being. Regarding informed choice:

- Top management teams that use participative decision making—creating more informed choice—have more effective decisions and better organizational performance.[28]
- Top management teams that share more information, collaborate more, and jointly make decisions report better organizational performance and attract and retain talented employees more easily.[29]
- Team performance is greater when members are involved sooner and in more depth in decision making.[30]
- When people are involved in decision making, they have greater commitment.[31]
- The earlier that people are involved in decision making regarding a change process, the more likely they are to accept it and the better they adjust to it.[32]
- Top management teams that create more informed choice have better working relationships between management and employees as well as among employees.[33]
- When team members are involved in decision making, they have higher job satisfaction.[34]

- Their satisfaction increases as they become involved earlier and in more depth.[35]

Regarding accountability:

- When teams and individuals have greater accountability, they perform better.[36]
- When there is greater accountability, teams seem to consider more information and review it more carefully.[37]
- When people are accountable for the reasoning they used to reach a decision, they make more accurate decisions.[38]

One problem teams face is that they don't give enough consideration to information that only one member has. Teams tend to give more weight to information that several members—the more the better—bring to the table. But when teams do incorporate one-holder information into solutions, they make better decisions. That's because they use all the information available to them, not just the information that team members are familiar with. Teams that are accountable for the process they use to make their decisions are better able to use all the information available to them and make higher-quality decisions.[39]

Accountability also affects team member relationships.

- People who are held accountable make less biased decisions and ones that are less judgmental.[40]
- When people are accountable for how they reach their decisions, they make fewer inappropriate inferences and attributions about the attitudes and personalities of others.[41]

Compassion

Compassion is the fifth core value—and the emotional glue that holds all five core values together. Compassion has three parts. When you operate from compassion

- You are aware of the pain that people you work with face.
- You internally connect to their pain, cognitively and emotionally.
- You respond to the pain.

When I say *pain*, I'm talking about the daily frustrations people encounter, the emotionally wrenching decisions they need to make, and the stress they endure as a result. Compassion means temporarily suspending judgment so that you can genuinely understand others and appreciate their situation. It doesn't mean taking responsibility for solving other people's problems or pitying them.

Without compassion, the mutual learning approach feels hollow and robotic. People see you as just going through the motions, using the right words but not seeming genuine. But when you're compassionate, others experience you as being genuinely concerned and supportive. Even when you have to make tough decisions that negatively affect them, they feel that you have a spirit of generosity.

Compassion affects how you use the other core values. When you operate with compassion

- You're *transparent* not simply because you want to tell people what you think but because you appreciate their need to make sense of your behavior.
- You're *curious* about others not because you want to use their responses to show them how they're wrong but because you want to appreciate the situation from their perspective.
- You create *informed choice* for others not only because informed choice leads to greater commitment but because informed choice is a fundamental way of respecting others.
- You hold others *accountable* not because you believe that people won't follow through unless you do but because accountability is a way of honoring one's commitment to others and the results you jointly seek to achieve.

Being compassionate doesn't mean rescuing people—doing things for them that they could and should do for themselves. Nor does it mean avoiding transparency and accountability, and preventing informed choices, by ducking important but difficult conversations or decisions because you don't want people to feel bad. What compassion *does* mean is suspending judgment about others even as you hold each other accountable.

The first client group to which I introduced the core value of compassion were high-tech leader-engineers developing computer chips. Their organization had come to dominate its market though logical, analytic research and development. Its culture drove hard. I was concerned that this hard-nosed crew would summarily dismiss the whole idea of compassion. To my surprise—and great relief—they applauded compassion. They had seen how focusing purely on logic without compassion led to a workplace in which strained, mistrustful relationships made working together more difficult.

I have purposely chosen *compassion* over words like *empathy* or *understanding* because I want to highlight the value of the heart—or more precisely, the feelings—in decision making. Until recently, many people (myself included) believed that thoughts and feelings were in a battle over the quality of decision making. Thoughts represented logic and analysis, which we considered the pure elements of decision making. Feelings were merely distractions or contaminations of thought. In that model, considering what people were feeling only compromised the quality of purely logic-based decision making. Some did believe that integrating thoughts and feelings into decision making could generate better decisions than focusing only on logic, but the research wasn't there to support their views. Now it's clear that, under certain conditions, they were right.

Recent research shows that leaders and teams are more effective when they pay attention to thoughts and feelings.[42] The seventeenth-century mathematician and philosopher Blaise Pascal was ahead of his time when he said, "The heart has its reasons, which reason does not know. . . . We know truth, not only by the reason, but also by the heart."

The Power of Compassion

Although philosophies and religions have extolled the virtues of compassion for thousands of years, researchers have just recently begun to identify how compassion at work makes a difference:

- Negotiators who have low compassion have less desire to work with each other in the future and generate fewer joint gains.[43]
- People who respond compassionately reduce punishing behaviors that can create further negative consequences.[44]
- Early findings also suggest that compassion can increase commitment to the organization.[45]

In my own experience working with leaders, when leaders respond with compassion they improve their working relationships and their own individual satisfaction. When leaders demonstrate concern about others' needs and suffering, defensive behavior and unproductive conflict both decline. Leaders are able to learn more about the situation. All of this contributes to increased trust.

Compassion Versus Distancing

Some people are naturally more compassionate than others. But for everyone, it's harder to be compassionate when feeling frustrated, disappointed, or annoyed. Those feelings make it tempting to distance yourself from others and their pain by telling yourself that they don't deserve compassion. As Diane Berke writes, "The major block to compassion is the judgment in our minds. Judgment is the mind's primary tool of separation."[46] Here are some judgmental messages we tend to think or convey:

Your suffering isn't that serious. When you tell yourself that the other person's suffering isn't serious, you're saying that the person doesn't deserve compassion. When a team member says, "I'm totally overwhelmed with work," are you dismissively thinking, "Be glad you have a job in this economy," "Get over it, we're all in the same boat," or "Stop whining and wasting my time"? When someone says, "I can't get any cooperation from the other division," do you think, "That's what we pay you to do—make it happen"? Suffering isn't a competition. Another person's suffering doesn't have to exceed yours for you to be compassionate.

You contributed to your problem. In this version of judging, only the faultless person earns your compassion. If someone didn't take complete initiative, didn't respond as effectively as possible, or didn't seek help early enough, they don't get your compassion. But most of us contribute at least somewhat (if not largely) to our own challenges. If you extend compassion only to those who have made no contribution to their problems, you'll exclude most of the people you work with—and yourself. Consider instead broadening or deepening your compassion so that you can feel for others even when—or especially when—they have brought on or worsened their problem.

You're acting like a victim. People act like victims when they discount their ability to help themselves or blame others for their problems. It doesn't mean they're not suffering, it only means they don't see the extent of their ability and responsibility to do something about a problem. If you believe that someone is acting like a victim—even if that's not the case—and you get angry at them or feel pity for them, you won't be able to respond with compassion. Instead, consider being compassionate even if the person is acting like a victim.

You haven't shown compassion for me, so I'm not giving it to you. With this judgment you require others to make the first move. Until they show you compassion, you will withhold it from them. Sometimes we withhold compassion from people simply because they are like other people who haven't shown us compassion in the past.

When I was growing up, I was regularly frustrated by my teachers and the school administrators. I was an excellent student, but I was frustrated with how teachers taught, with school policies that didn't sufficiently take into account student interests, and with the lack of responsiveness to student concerns. I found myself regularly trying to create organizational change in my schools—and was just as regularly rebuffed. The administrators dismissed my requests; they showed little compassion for my concerns. On the positive side, my frustration with these administrators motivated me to become an organizational psychologist.

Fast-forward fifteen years. I was a professor teaching school superintendents and principals in an executive education program. My topic was managing change and conflict. I remember looking out at my class of school administrators and thinking, *Finally, the tables are turned. Now you're in my school and I've got the power.* I had quickly distanced myself from the people I was there to help even though none of them had done anything to me. As a result, they didn't get the learning or compassion they deserved—and my evaluations showed it. Looking back, I realized that payback was more on my mind than compassion.

The assumption that people must *earn* your compassion is always destructive. Avoid the temptation to think that it's not enough for people to be human and interdependent with you; they must also meet your standards before you will grace them with a compassionate response. If someone has to earn it from you, it's not compassion.

When you assume you have to choose between showing compassion or holding someone accountable, you get stuck in either-or thinking. The mutual learning approach enables you to get unstuck by using both-and thinking. Showing compassion doesn't mean giving someone a free pass. You can show compassion at the same time you hold people accountable for their actions.

Responding with Compassion

In a meeting with one or more members of your leadership team, assuming you've connected to the pain others seem to be feeling, how do you respond? Do you ignore it and simply refocus on the agenda? Do you tell them things will be easier if they focus on the positive? Do you acknowledge that this is hard for people and then move on? Or do you temporarily—even briefly—put aside your agenda and find out how they are feeling and what they need from you, if anything? All but the last response distance you from people who are suffering.

Responding means talking with others about their pain in an effort to help. Responding doesn't mean eliminating their pain or solving their problem for them. It means understanding their situation and expressing your concern for them.

But even those who are feeling compassionate have a set of messages that can get in the way of responding with compassion. For example:

If I'm compassionate, they will think I agree with them. Some leaders worry that if they show someone compassion, that person will think agreement goes along with it. But you can be compassionate even as you disagree or can't support what the person has done. It's perfectly reasonable to show your concern for someone at the same time you express concern. You might say something like, "I don't agree with how you went about doing this, because I think you contributed to the situation you're in. But I feel for you. You're in a really tough situation."

If I'm compassionate, I can't hold the person accountable. Believing that if you show compassion you won't be able to insist on accountability creates a situation in which you must choose between the two. But this is a false choice. You can do both. In fact, if you don't hold people accountable when it's appropriate, you risk taking on their responsibilities.

If I'm compassionate, I could open up a can of worms. Imagine that in your meeting with Jason, one of your direct reports, he mentions that his role as corporate spokesperson is becoming overwhelming. You respond with compassion, saying that you've noticed he looks tired and that you're worried about him. Hearing your compassion, Jason tells you that the daily attacks from the media and activist groups combined with the organization's shifting strategy for dealing with the public are making it impossible for his team to get anything else done. All of this is taking a heavy toll on his team and him. Some people are showing signs of burnout, others are reporting being depressed, and Jason has starting taking antidepressants on the advice of his physician. As he tells you this, you're feeling bad for

Jason. At the same time you're thinking, "Have I gotten myself in too deep on this? I'm his boss, not a therapist. Besides, I can't afford to have Jason check out. The organization needs him now." But you can respond with compassion without telling him to take the week off and let you handle the troubles. For instance, you might start by saying something like, "Jason, I'm really sorry to hear this and I'm really glad you told me. I know that you and your team have been dealing with a hostile public and I get that it's taking a toll. I want to make sure that you and your team have the support you need so you can get the job done without continuing to pay a price with your mental health. Can we talk about how to do that?"

Sometimes leaders feel for others, but they worry that if they respond compassionately, they might encourage people to open up about issues that are better left undiscussed. It's natural at times to wish you didn't know something. But not knowing doesn't make the problem or its impact go away. By being compassionate and curious, you learn about challenges that already exist—and you get the information necessary to support others in resolving the problem before it has a chance to turn into a disastrous collapse.

Sometimes leaders worry that being compassionate will take them into conversations they're not qualified to deal with. People might talk to you about strained relations with their children or spouse, or about financial trouble or mental illness. The good news is that you can be compassionate even if you have no expertise about the situation that is causing the person's suffering. That's because compassion isn't about solving problems. All you may need to do is listen, share your concern for the person, and extend an appropriate offer to help.

ASSUMPTIONS OF THE MUTUAL LEARNING MINDSET

Along with the core values, the mutual learning mindset leads you to operate from a set of assumptions. Take a moment now to look back at Figure 3.1 to review the set of values you just covered and to note the five assumptions.

Assumption 1: *I have information; so do others.* With this assumption you recognize that on any topic, others are likely to have relevant information. Unlike the unilateral control mindset, in which you assume you have all the information you need, in mutual learning you assume that because people have different responsibilities and experiences on the team, they will naturally have different information. That information may be the same as or consistent with the information you have, it may be complementary, or it may even be at odds with your current information.

Assumption 2: *Each of us sees things others don't.* If people may have different information because of their different responsibilities and experiences, then it makes sense that each individual may see a situation differently from other team members. Even when team members are in the same meetings and hear the same information, the mutual learning mindset recognizes that each may see different implications or consequences, or assign different value to the information.

Assumption 3: *Differences are opportunities for learning.* With the mutual learning mindset, team members' different information, experiences, and views become the basis for team learning that leads to better results and relationships. You're eager to discover how people see things differently from you because you recognize that it's the beginning of a creative process that will lead to better solutions. With a unilateral control mindset, you're either reluctant to explore differences because you know you're right and see nothing to be gained from it, or you're willing to engage others only in order to show they are wrong.

Assumption 4: *People may disagree with me and still have pure motives.* Because you assume that different views are natural and lead to better results, you can have significant disagreements within your team and still believe that each member is approaching the situation with pure motives. As a result, you're not spending time and energy wondering about and trying to protect against the possible harmful motives of other team members the way you would with the unilateral control mindset.

When you operate from this assumption, something wonderful happens—the organization contains fewer jerks. This isn't a naive mind game in which you wish away people you don't like. Instead, when you change your mindset, it changes your behavior—which can change how others respond to you. You know that famous bumper-sticker quote from Gandhi—the one that says, "Be the change you want to see in the world"? He didn't actually say that, but he did say something even more on point for our discussion: "If we could change ourselves, the tendencies in the world would also change. As a man changes his own nature, so does the attitude of the world change towards him.... We need not wait to see what others do."[47]

When you operate from this assumption, something wonderful happens—the organization contains fewer jerks.

Assumption 5: *I may be contributing to the problem.* In the mutual learning mindset, you recognize that you may be an active part of the very problems that you're complaining about. You see the working relationships with your team as a complex set of causal relationships rather than as a one-way street in which others act ineffectively and you respond effectively. Just as other team members may be thinking and acting ineffectively, so too may you. You recognize that others' ineffective behavior may actually be a result of (and reaction to) your ineffective mindset and behavior, and you realize your reactions to others' ineffective behaviors can either aid or impede mutual learning.

In a unilateral control mindset, only others need to change. In a mutual learning mindset, you realize that each team member plays a role that prevents the team from achieving its goals. Even members who watch or withdraw as the team struggles contribute by virtue of their silence. As a team, all members share accountability for the results and all contribute to them. Consequently, you appreciate that the whole team—including you—may need to change.

MUTUAL LEARNING BEHAVIORS

Mutual learning behaviors convert the mutual learning mindset into action. Using a mutual learning mindset, you can generate behaviors that aren't possible from a unilateral control mindset. You're able to share all the relevant information about a situation, find out what others are thinking, test assumptions that you and others are making, develop solutions that address people's interests, raise what might have been undiscussable issues, and jointly design next steps. Figure 3.2 summarizes the eight behaviors.

RESULTS OF MUTUAL LEARNING

The results you get with a mutual learning mindset are the opposite of those you get with unilateral control—but they still fall into the same three types: team performance, working relationships, and well-being. See Figure 3.3.

Better Team Performance

What are most leaders thinking when they create a high-performing team? That the team exists to create results that individuals alone can't achieve separately. With mutual learning behaviors, your team improves performance in several ways: higher-quality decisions, increased innovation, faster decision-plus-implementation, and lower costs.

Higher-Quality Decisions and Greater Innovation

It's difficult to know at the time whether your team's decisions are good ones. Often the answer depends on factors that your team can't predict or on information you don't yet have. But smarter teams have ways of working that increase the chance of making good decisions

Behavior

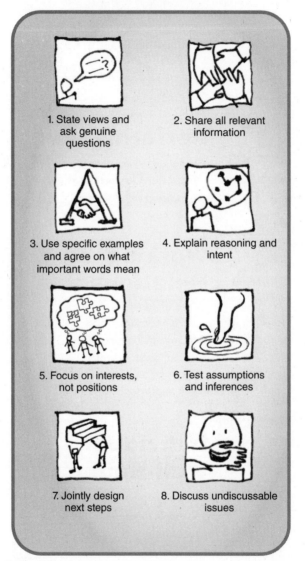

1. State views and ask genuine questions

2. Share all relevant information

3. Use specific examples and agree on what important words mean

4. Explain reasoning and intent

5. Focus on interests, not positions

6. Test assumptions and inferences

7. Jointly design next steps

8. Discuss undiscussable issues

Figure 3.2. Behaviors Generated by the Mutual Learning Mindset

Source: Roger Schwarz & Associates; used with permission.

Results

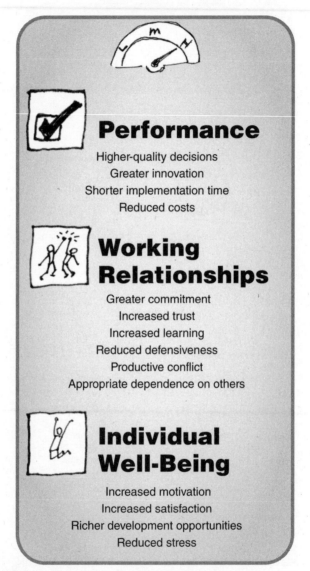

Performance

Higher-quality decisions
Greater innovation
Shorter implementation time
Reduced costs

**Working
Relationships**

Greater commitment
Increased trust
Increased learning
Reduced defensiveness
Productive conflict
Appropriate dependence on others

**Individual
Well-Being**

Increased motivation
Increased satisfaction
Richer development opportunities
Reduced stress

Figure 3.3. Results of a Mutual Learning Mindset
Source: Roger Schwarz & Associates; used with permission.

even when the situation is uncertain. They are able to create a common pool of accurate information and a shared understanding of the situation they face. Members understand the different stakeholder needs that have to be met and so can craft solutions that address these needs.

Smarter teams also make decisions that are innovative. They create something new and original. Smarter teams are able to make innovative decisions because they're aware of and can challenge the assumptions that have constrained past decisions. To raise and explore these assumptions, team members rely on mutual trust.[48]

Shorter Implementation Time

Some leaders worry that using mutual learning means taking more time to make decisions. My response is, "More time than what?" Is it more than having a twenty-minute meeting with your team to make a decision, after which several team members individually close your office door and take twenty minutes each trying to convince you that the team decision won't work? Is it more than quickly implementing a decision only to learn that the implementation plan has to be reworked several times because team members didn't share important information or because the plan was based on incorrect assumptions that the team didn't check out? As I noted in Chapter Two, the finish time isn't when your team has made a decision—it's when the decision has been successfully implemented.

Smart teams shorten the time between identifying a problem or opportunity and successfully implementing their decision. Teams often try to save time by shortening their time to make a decision. My father, an executive who was an engineer by training, hung these words above his large wooden workbench in our basement: "If you don't have time to do it right the first time, how will you find time to do it the second time?" Mutual learning behaviors reduce the overall time of decision making and implementation by addressing issues that team members know will become problems if they aren't addressed before implementation.

Reduced Costs

Mutual learning teams find ways to reduce costs while maintaining or increasing value. Sometimes reduced costs result from shorter implementation time and more innovative solutions. Other times the cost savings are the purpose of the work itself.

At MCUS Corporation (the name of the organization has been changed at the request of the client), an energy company I worked with, an operational support services team had been trying unsuccessfully for years to have its accounts payable groups pay its vendors using an early-pay discount program. Many vendors were willing to accept less money if they could get it sooner, but most of the accounts payable groups seemed surprisingly uninterested in pursuing the savings. After working with several accounts payable groups the operational services team had labeled resistant to early pay, the team was able to craft an agreement with them. They accomplished this by getting curious about why the accounts payable people were not interested in early pay discounts, sharing relevant information they had not previously shared with accounts payable, and making sure the solution addressed accounts payable's needs. As a result, the organization saved $1.3 million during the first year.

Better Team Working Relationships

The second area of results is team working relationships. Here mutual learning generates greater commitment, increased trust, increased team learning, and appropriate dependence on others. It also reduces defensiveness and makes conflict more productive. When your team has this kind of working relationship, you know that members want to work with each other and that working together produces better performance.

Greater Commitment

Mutual learning behaviors generate greater commitment to the team's decisions and to the team itself. By *commitment*, I mean promising to take action to support something. Creating team commitment is a simple—if not easy—process. A team becomes committed to a decision when team members believe that their interests have been considered. When you operate from a mutual learning mindset, you're curious about others' interests and jointly design solutions that address them.

Increased Trust

Trust provides the foundation for teams, but you can't build it directly. Trust develops when team members rely on each other, take risks with each other, and expect things of each other—and find that their reliance and risks pay off, and their best expectations are fulfilled. Initially, team members may grant each other some level of trust, but ultimately it must be earned.

The mutual learning core values and assumptions set the stage for increased trust. You operate from a spirit of generosity when you assume that team members can disagree with you and still have pure motives and when you assume that differences are opportunities for learning. When you combine this with transparency and compassion, you can trust that team members will tell you what they think in a way that is helpful. You can also trust that members will take your needs into account, even if you're not there to represent them. With increased accountability, you can also trust that members will follow through on their commitments. When there is trust, members feel psychologically safe. They're willing to be vulnerable with each other and can create more innovative solutions.

Increased Learning, Reduced Defensiveness, and More Productive Conflict

Researchers have suggested that an organization's greatest competitive advantage is the speed at which it learns.[49] The faster your leadership team learns, the faster it can anticipate or respond to changing conditions, both outside and inside the organization.

The trust that your mutual learning team generates creates a safer environment for your team to learn.[50] Team members see their team as the shared vehicle for driving results and they constantly look for ways of improving the ride. They are willing play with ideas, raise difficult issues, and otherwise make themselves vulnerable; they know that other team members will not put them down or retaliate.

When your team operates from a mutual learning mindset, it can discuss difficult issues *in the team* without members becoming defensive. I've seen such teams openly discuss and deal with how some team members' performance is hindering the entire team's ability to achieve its goals, how certain team members aren't held as accountable as others, and how all team members are colluding to avoid taking initiative. In a health care organization, I watched the clinical leadership team—the team responsible for all medical care in the organization—ask its leader, the chief medical officer, whether he was being pushed out of the organization by the executive vice president—who was sitting next to him in the meeting and who had been taking on some of the CMO's responsibilities. The CMO's transparent and nondefensive responses enabled the team to understand the situation more fully and address their concerns sufficiently so that the team could figure out how they would lead, given the new leadership structure.

When your team operates from a mutual learning mindset, it can discuss difficult issues in the team without members becoming defensive.

This level of mutual trust and understanding makes it easier to engage in productive conflict. Simply put, team members get into conflicts when two or more members pursue actions or solutions that are inconsistent with each other. A team with a mutual learning mindset understands that conflict is natural and inevitable. They expect that members will have different views on issues and they see that as strength because they know how to use those differences to create solutions that are smarter than those devised by any individual. This productive use of conflict creates the learning that leads to better decisions. Overall and over time, working relationships strengthen within the team.

Appropriate Dependence on Others

With mutual learning, team members depend appropriately on others. Team members manage their working relationships directly with each other, rather than requiring someone else to serve as intermediary.

This was an important element for John Haley's leadership team, which has also appeared in Chapters One and Two. After mutual learning became the norm, John no longer had his business unit or functional leaders coming to him after meetings, expressing concerns about other team members or decisions. Instead, members took responsibility for addressing their own concerns, either one-on-one or in the full group as appropriate. This in turn got all the information out on the table and reduced the number of meetings needed to resolve an issue.

Greater Individual Well-Being

In teams where mutual learning prevails, team members—including the team leader—find the overall team experience satisfying rather than frustrating. They find the work motivating, enjoyable, and not too stressful.

It's worth repeating: members find *doing the work itself* motivating. The work gives them a chance to use their range of skills, allows for autonomy, and lets them see how they make a difference.[51] As a result, doing the work well is self-reinforcing. Although team members expect rewards for performing well, they see rewards as recognition for good work, not the motivation for producing it.

Finally, when teams are smart, members experience a healthy level and kind of stress—the kind that comes from taking on challenging goals and that generates peak performance.

HOW MUTUAL LEARNING REINFORCES ITSELF

The wonderful thing about the mutual learning mindset is that the more you use it, the more you strengthen it. As the arrows bordering Figure 3.4 suggest, when you use mutual learning, others typically start to respond more positively to you. It becomes easier to make better team decisions that the team is committed to. Team members who used to seem clueless or stubborn now seem to have something valuable to offer. Team members are able to productively integrate their different views so that the team feels better about how they are working together. Challenging people seem less challenging. Teams are systems and when one part of the system changes—whether that's you or other team members—it creates change in the larger system. This is the essence of the of the Gandhi quote I mentioned earlier.

IS UNILATERAL CONTROL STILL AN OPTION?

If you're thinking that a full-blown mutual learning approach is sometimes unnecessary or even inappropriate, you're right—but the mutual learning *mindset* is still relevant. At a fire, for example, fire-fighters need to respond to orders; they don't have time to discuss how they will coordinate. But issuing directives for others to follow doesn't necessarily mean you're using a unilateral control approach. It is a unilateral control approach only if your team doesn't have opportunities before and after to discuss the conditions under which directives should prevail.

My colleagues and I have helped police and fire organizations use mutual learning. At a fire or police action, teams use what I call directive leadership just like other organizations. But they use mutual learning outside these situations, including debriefing the directive situations to improve collaboration.

If you're thinking you sometimes need to make an immediate decision and don't have time to involve others, you're also correct. That's not necessarily unilateral control either, as long as you explain your decisions afterward and ask for feedback.

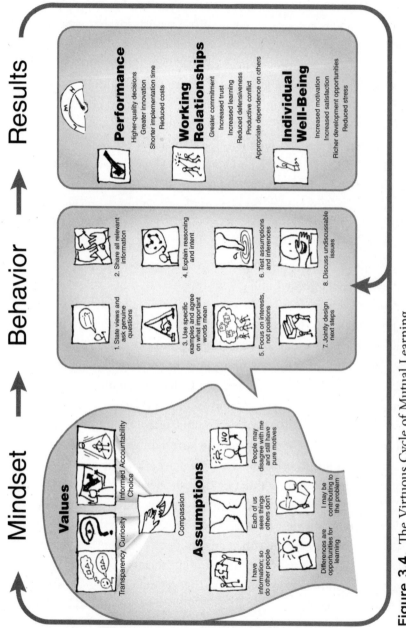

Mindset → **Behavior** → **Results**

Values
Transparency Curiosity Informed Accountability
                         Choice

Compassion

Assumptions
I have information; so do other people

Differences are opportunities for learning

Each of us sees things others don't

People may disagree with me and still have pure motives

I may be contributing to the problem

1. State views and ask genuine questions
2. Share all relevant information
3. Use specific examples and agree on what important words mean
4. Explain reasoning and intent
5. Focus on interests, not positions
6. Test assumptions and inferences
7. Jointly design next steps
8. Discuss undiscussable issues

Performance
Higher-quality decisions
Greater innovation
Shorter implementation time
Reduced costs

Working Relationships
Greater commitment
Increased trust
Increased learning
Reduced defensiveness
Productive conflict
Appropriate dependence on others

Individual Well-Being
Increased motivation
Increased satisfaction
Richer development opportunities
Reduced stress

Figure 3.4. The Virtuous Cycle of Mutual Learning

Source: Roger Schwarz & Associates; used with permission.

And a lot of situations are so routine that you don't have to actively use a mutual learning approach. You don't have to be transparent about why you're asking your direct reports for their quarterly numbers by Friday when you're just reminding them of the usual due date. If it's a standard procedure, you've already shared your reasoning at some point in the past. But if you're changing the reporting deadline, mutual learning requires being transparent about what's different this quarter that leads you to shift the deadline and checking to see if that creates any problems for your direct reports.

Of course, if you *mostly* find yourself in situations where time is too short to get information from others before making a decision or you have to issue directives instead of getting input, you've probably deceived yourself into believing that you have to use a unilateral control approach.

Using mutual learning effectively means that you use the approach to the degree it's needed in a given situation. In a business context, in general your need for it increases as the situation becomes less routine, the stakes become higher, emotions run higher, points of view increasingly differ, or something unexpected happens. Even when you don't actively need to use specific mutual learning *behaviors*, you are still operating from a mutual learning *mindset*, ready to engage specific behaviors as soon as you need them.

Remember that when you use a mutual learning approach you're still concerned about winning, but you have a different way of understanding what it means to win. The *win, don't lose* value of unilateral control is part of a mindset that holds your views as right and those with different views as wrong. It puts winning above seeking truth and leads you to dismiss, belittle, or tear down others who see things differently. Even when you win, it creates losses—not only for others, but for you. In mutual learning, winning means generating valid information and seeking the truth. This trumps getting your way because you can.

In many of the organizations my colleagues and I work with, the work centers on engineering, medicine, or other areas of science.

Although they provide very different products and services, they all work from a common approach: the scientific method, which basically involves solving problems by identifying hypotheses and testing them by collecting and analyzing experimental data in a rigorous way. Every engineer, scientist, and physician relies on the scientific method to make sense in technical situations. It's the shared set of ground rules that scientists of all stripes use to resolve technical conflicts. To the extent that the scientific method leads people to reach conclusions that some had hypothesized and others had not, you could say that there are winners and losers. But if you believe in the scientific method as your way of discovering technical truth, whatever conclusion you reach is a win, because it is based on sound process. It's the same with mutual learning.

In mutual learning, you win when you and others develop a solution that is based on all the relevant information and meets as many stakeholder interests as possible.

EXTENDING MUTUAL LEARNING TO THE WHOLE TEAM

If you as an individual develop a mutual learning mindset and use it to shape your behaviors, you can improve your performance, the way you work with others, and even your own well-being. But you've probably noticed that this chapter has already shifted the discussion here and there to a broader goal of making mutual learning the mindset shared by the team as a whole. That's how you'll really improve your team's performance, the way your team works together, and your team members' well-being. Your goal should be to design a team and its environment to maximize its mutual learning potential.

A Team Mindset of Mutual Learning

How you think is how you will lead. But in a team, it's more accurate to say how *we* think is how *we* lead. That's because in mutual learning everyone is accountable for the team's effectiveness, not just you. And it's not only your mindset that makes the team more or less effective. If it were, developing your team would be easy. All you would need to do is change your thinking and—voilà—your team would be magically transformed.

If you're the only person acting from this mindset, you can influence how your team works together and the results it gets, but your influence will be limited. When you're working directly with your team, you'll be able to use your mindset and skill set to raise the quality of problem solving and decision making in the team. You'll be able to help team members explain more of what they are thinking, test their assumptions, and resolve conflicts and solve problems so they meet the team members' different needs.

But if you're the only one who understands mutual learning, team members will constantly need your help and won't be able to do it without you. They won't be able to think differently and consequently act differently on their own. Because team members haven't internalized the mutual learning mindset, when you're not present they will revert to their normal approach.

To benefit fully from mutual learning, the whole team needs to share the mindset. To achieve the mutual learning results the team as a whole needs to be transparent and curious. It needs to create informed choice, be accountable, and practice compassion. Everyone needs to show up assuming that they have some of the information but not all of it; that others see things that they may not; that people can disagree and still have pure motives; that differences are opportunities for learning; and that they may be contributing to a problem.

You will also need your team's help. Remember that part of operating from a unilateral control mindset includes being blind to the fact that you're using unilateral control. The good news is that others around you can clearly see when you are using it. That means you—and everyone else on the team—needs others to help identify when unilateral control is in play, so they can shift back to mutual learning. It's much easier for your team members to see unilateral control in others than to produce mutual learning behaviors themselves.

Team Behaviors

A shared team mindset enables shared mutual learning behaviors. Like you, your team needs to use them consistently. At the same time, if team members simply learn the behaviors without understanding, appreciating, and internalizing the mindset that drives them, their work will be hollow and ineffectual.

Many leadership teams never get the results they seek because they focus primarily—sometimes exclusively—on simply changing behavior. Because the team doesn't change the mindset that is driving their old behaviors, their old unilateral control mindset trumps any new behaviors that seek to change unilateral control.

For your team to consistently use mutual learning behaviors, members need to agree explicitly to expect these behaviors of each other, whether they are working as a full team or in subgroups. When the team explicitly commits to using mutual learning behaviors and expects team members to use them, the behaviors become an important and powerful part of the team norms. Without this explicit agreement, members may consider the behaviors valuable but not use them.

For your team to benefit from mutual learning behavior, members also need to give each other feedback in the moment. When a team member is stating a conclusion without explaining the thinking that led to it, other team members need to point this out at the time it occurs and ask the person to explain the reasoning. When a team member is making untested assumptions, other team members need to point that out and ask the person to test the assumptions.

The feedback is necessary because, again, everyone is typically blind to using the unilateral control mindset and behavior. Everyone needs others to help recognize this behavior and self-correct. This is part of the accountability of shared leadership.

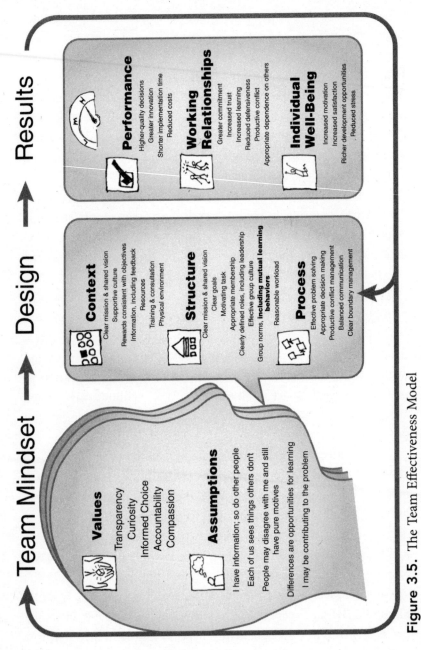

Team Mindset → Design → Results

Team Mindset

Values
Transparency
Curiosity
Informed Choice
Accountability
Compassion

Assumptions
I have information; so do other people
Each of us sees things others don't
People may disagree with me and still have pure motives
Differences are opportunities for learning
I may be contributing to the problem

Design

Context
Clear mission & shared vision
Supportive culture
Rewards consistent with objectives
Information, including feedback
Resources
Training & consultation
Physical environment

Structure
Clear mission & shared vision
Clear goals
Motivating task
Appropriate membership
Clearly defined roles, including leadership
Effective group culture
Group norms, including **mutual learning behaviors**
Reasonable workload

Process
Effective problem solving
Appropriate decision making
Productive conflict management
Balanced communication
Clear boundary management

Results

Performance
Higher-quality decisions
Greater innovation
Shorter implementation time
Reduced costs

Working Relationships
Greater commitment
Increased trust
Increased learning
Reduced defensiveness
Productive conflict
Appropriate dependence on others

Individual Well-Being
Increased motivation
Increased satisfaction
Richer development opportunities
Reduced stress

Figure 3.5. The Team Effectiveness Model
Source: Roger Schwarz & Associates; used with permission.

Team Design

Great potential lies in the fact that you can actually design any team with mutual learning in mind, and how you design it will affect its results. When I talk about *team design*, I'm referring to the structures and processes that your team uses to accomplish its work. Structures include such things as your team's mission and goals, as well as the roles that team members play in the team. Processes include such things as the methods your team uses for solving problems, making decisions, and resolving conflicts. You may also be able to design or influence the context in which the team functions to support the mutual learning approach.

Figure 3.5 shows the Team Effectiveness Model. While the mutual learning approach focuses on individual mindset, behavior, and results, the Team Effectiveness Model focuses on the team as a whole, including its collective mindset, design, and team results. Note that in the Team Effectiveness Model, the mutual learning behaviors are included in group norms under "Structure."

If you design your team congruent with mutual learning mindset and behavior, you make it much easier to achieve the results you see in the figure. But if you design your team so it's at odds with mutual learning, the misalignment between your design and the mindset and team behavior will create conflicts and make it harder to achieve them.

The challenge for you and your team is to design the team with the same mindset you use to design your behavior. If you use a unilateral control mindset in challenging situations, chances are you've designed at least part of your team using that same mindset: embedded in your team design are one or more of the unilateral control core values and assumptions—even if that wasn't your intent.

CHAPTER 4

Getting the Puzzle Pieces on the Table
Mutual Learning Behaviors 1–4

I t's one thing to say you value transparency, curiosity, and accountability, along with informed choice and compassion. But it's
another thing to act that way. So what do you actually say and do
to walk the talk?

I've developed a list of eight behaviors based on research and
my more than thirty years of helping leaders and their teams
improve their results. Over the years I've tightened and tuned it (an
earlier version contained sixteen behaviors!) systematically down to
essentials. Each behavior makes a unique contribution and together
they are more than the sum of their parts. Even though I have
numbered the behaviors, you won't be using them in one specific
order. Each behavior is like a dance step that becomes part of a
larger routine.

Behaviors 2 through 4 are subsets of Behavior 1: they represent
specific things you do when you use Behavior 1 (see Figure 4.1).
They're the focus of this chapter; Chapter Five explores the other four
behaviors.

Behavior

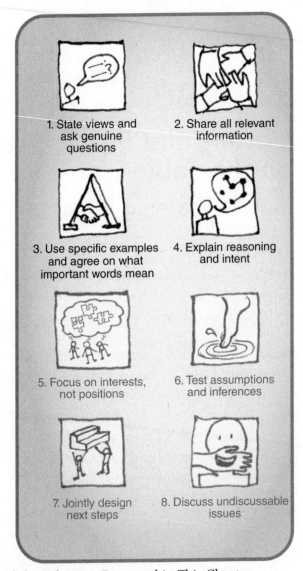

Figure 4.1. Behaviors Discussed in This Chapter
Source: Roger Schwarz & Associates; used with permission.

BEHAVIOR 1: STATE VIEWS AND ASK GENUINE QUESTIONS

When you state your views and ask genuine questions, you're automatically transparent and curious.

WHAT YOU CAN DO

Next time you're in a team meeting trying to solve a problem (not just giving updates), keep track of the number of times people make statements and ask questions. Each time someone speaks, put a tally mark next to "make statement" or "ask question," or put a mark next to each if they do both. At the end of the meeting, calculate the percentage of comments that are statements and the percentage that are questions. To see how you contribute to this team dynamic, you can keep a separate tally of your own statements and questions.

Unfortunately, if yours is like most leadership teams I've observed, you'll see that team members do a lot more of telling others what they think than of asking about others' views. And this troubling observation will hold even if you count false questions as questions.

Watch more closely as your team tries to solve a problem, and you'll probably see something like this: One member starts by stating what he thinks is the problem. A second member makes a statement, either agreeing or stating that the problem is different. Then other members make their comments. As you watch the discussion unfold, you think to yourself, *"Team members aren't really building on each other's comments. Sometimes their comments don't seem related to each other. And some of the comments seem off track."* By the end of the meeting, you may have a decision, but you probably also have a nagging feeling that the team didn't get all the information out on the table and there is less than full commitment to implement it. You may leave the meeting wondering what some people really think. That's what happens when everyone states only their views and doesn't ask questions.

Raise Your Curiosity, Don't Lower Your Passion

If you realize that you and your team aren't as curious as you could be, raise your curiosity; don't lower your transparency or passion. That is, it does no good to suddenly start asking a lot of questions while saying very little about your own views. As a leader, you have strong views on issues and people expect that. If you start watering down your views or holding back what you believe, your team will lose the benefit of your perspective and you'll be frustrated with yourself. Instead, combine your own passionate statements with curiosity. You can express your own views as passionately as you want, as long as you're equally curious about others' views. If you combine your passion with equal curiosity, you will engage others and be engaged yourself.

> *You can express your own views as passionately as you want, as long as you're equally curious about others' views.*

After you state your view, ask a question to learn what others think about what you've said. Depending on what the team is trying to accomplish and what you need to understand, you might ask, "Does anyone have any different information?" or "Is anyone else facing the same problem?" or "What problems do you see with the solution I'm suggesting?"

By asking a question after you state your view, you move the conversation forward and keep it focused. When you ask, "What problems does anyone see with this solution?" you immediately increase the chance that the next person who speaks responds to your question. If each person does the same thing, you move from a series of potentially unrelated comments to a problem-solving meeting. Asking genuine questions also increases the chance that you'll learn that people see things differently than you do. That's especially important when you're working with people who have less power than you and may be concerned about giving you bad news.

Of course, you don't have to also ask a question every time you state your views; use your judgment. Just keep in mind that combining transparency and curiosity is what will do most to create a common pool of information and understanding.

Make Sure Your Questions Are Genuine

Not all questions are created equal. If your questions are genuine, you'll engage others. If your questions aren't genuine, you'll turn people off. False, often called rhetorical, questions can feel good to ask. They're a way to score some quick—and often clever—verbal points in a frustrating situation. But rhetorical questions seek to make a point or to make people do something, not to come up with a real answer.

When you ask rhetorical questions, you embed your point of view in the question without being transparent, and you're not really curious. Rhetorical questions enable you to convey your views in ways that are hard to challenge but still require others to defend their views. "You don't really think that solution will work, do you?" basically asserts that the speaker doesn't think the solution will work and that the other person should instantly agree. It demands that the listener cave at once or defend the allegedly untenable position. In one organization I worked with, the CEO was well-known for demanding, "Who the hell thought that was a good idea?" It wasn't exactly a conversation starter.

Rhetorical questions aren't transparent. They don't require you to be accountable for your view. They also feel like gotchas. They lead others to feel insulted, cornered, or discounted, making them inclined to check out of the conversation, resist your efforts, and trust you less. In short, if you use such questions, you lose those you're working with. That makes it harder to generate and implement good decisions that everyone can commit to. Test this for yourself: how do you react to rhetorical questions like the ones I've posed here?

We typically ask rhetorical questions when we're feeling frustrated with whoever is not agreeing with us. In short, we're usually thinking they don't understand the situation, are just plain wrong, have questionable motives, or all three.

How can you tell if your questions are genuine or not? If you answer yes to any of the following questions, the question you're about to ask isn't genuine.

- Do I already know the answer to my question?
- Am I asking the question to see if people will give the right (preferred) answer?
- Am I asking the question to make a point?

Apply the "You Idiot" Test

Another way to figure out if you're about to ask a nongenuine question is to apply what I call the "You Idiot" test. Here's how it works:

1. *Privately say to yourself the question you plan to ask.* For example, one of your direct reports has just told you he is going to be late on a project and significant additional costs will now be incurred in the upcoming fiscal year, the very outcome you were trying hard to avoid. You're tempted to respond, "Why do you think I asked you to make sure the work was done before the end of this fiscal year?"

2. *At the end of your private question, add the words "you idiot."* Now you're saying to yourself, "Why do you think I asked you to make sure the work was done before the end of this fiscal year, you idiot?" Actually, you can use any number of derogatory phrases.

You might prefer "you jerk," "you dummy," "you bozo," "you slacker."

3. *If the question still sounds natural with "you idiot" at its end, don't ask it.* It's really a statement—a pointed rhetorical question. Change the question to a transparent statement that appropriately expresses your frustration and a genuine question exploring how this situation occurred. You might say, "That really bothers me because it already puts next year's budget at risk. Help me understand; what happened to make project expenses spill over into next fiscal year?"

Open Your Gifts

Most of the time, you don't have to look for things to be curious about; team members offer them up as conversational gifts. In conversation (and e-mail and texting), team members offer gifts all the time. Unfortunately, it's easy to miss such gifts, often because it's scary to open them. But opening them can create better understanding, relationships, and results. So acknowledge the gift and get curious!

Some gifts are easy to recognize because they come wrapped in a compliment. But remember that the compliment is only the wrapping. When someone says, "You did a great job on that presentation to the directors," the gift is not the compliment. The gift is the opportunity for you to learn more about what the person thought was great. You open the gift when you respond by saying something like, "Thanks. Tell me, what was it that I did that you thought was great? I'm asking because I want to make sure to keep on doing it."

To open a gift, you do two things: acknowledge what the person said to you, and ask to hear more about it so you can better understand. Unfortunately, some of the best gifts you're given come horribly wrapped. They look bad, sound bad, and can even feel bad to open. Judging the gift by its wrapping makes it seem unpleasant to open these gifts—but leaving them packed is a real loss. Suppose one of your team members says, "I would have achieved all my goals this year if I had had full support from you." If you ignore the comment, simply disagree, or say, "We're here to talk about your performance, not mine," you've just rejected the gift you've been offered.

To open the gift, get curious. Try saying something like, "Tell me more; what are you thinking I was doing or not doing that didn't fully support you?" If you want to get better at recognizing and opening gifts, look for times when people say something that bothers you, confuses you, surprises you, or that you disagree with. Then start reminding yourself that these are opportunities for being curious and learning rather than for telling others they don't understand or are wrong.

Recall MCUS, the company whose accounts payable process was featured in Chapter Three. Owen Grant was the director who headed the team that was seeking to pay vendors early so as to secure discounts for MCUS. Paying just one vendor early could save $250,000 on a single invoice. Owen's team was responsible for managing more than $3 billion annually in spending, so the potential savings were significant. But when he tried to get support for early pay discounts, he encountered pushback from Phil Hughes, whose team was responsible for ensuring MCUS's construction projects were well managed and that the company had adequate cash on hand to meet its large capital obligations. At first, Owen couldn't understand how Phil could be against early pay discount—after all, it could be saving MCUS tens of millions of dollars annually.

Initially Owen got frustrated; then he decided to get curious. He talked with Phil for forty-five minutes, explaining what he was trying to do with early pay discounts and genuinely asking Phil what about the plan didn't work for him. First Owen learned that scheduling invoice payments was one way of managing the cash flows. But he still didn't understand how early pay discounts created a problem for Phil. So he asked Phil, "Does this not create cost savings for the projects?" Finally, Phil explained that early pay discounts weren't worth it. The 1–2 percent discount that MCUS received by paying early was much less than what MCUS would earn by delaying payments until the due dates. For Phil, the math simply didn't work.

Once Owen understood Phil's basic concern, he was able to address it. Owen had an e-mail from the finance group that showed that the cost of money was only .6 percent, much smaller than Phil had thought. When Phil understood that, he moved from objecting to the early pay discount program to offering to help Owen get support for it throughout the organization.

When you accept a person's gift—no matter how terribly wrapped—and respond with curiosity and compassion, you're giving a gift in return. In short, you are creating a safe space to talk about things that really matter. Creating this type of trust is priceless.

Curiosity Doesn't Mean Agreement

Some leaders worry that if they start to get curious and ask team members genuine questions, they may be seen as giving legitimacy to topics or solutions they don't agree with. But just because you're curious about what team members think doesn't mean you agree with them. If that's a concern, you can simply say, "I don't necessarily agree with you about this, but I'm trying to learn more about how you're seeing the situation. After I understand more, I may change my view." Stating your view and asking genuine questions raises the question *What do I share when I state my view?* The next few behaviors address that question.

BEHAVIOR 2: SHARE ALL RELEVANT INFORMATION

Being transparent means sharing all relevant information so that everyone involved has a common pool of information with which to make, understand, and implement decisions.

The key word is relevant. Relevant information is any information that might affect the decision that you or others make, how you go about making the decision, or your thoughts and feelings about it. Sharing relevant information doesn't necessarily mean that you say everything you know about a topic or everything that enters your mind during a conversation. Deciding what is relevant requires making judgments in each situation.

Unfortunately, in challenging situations, people often leave a significant gap between what they say and what they are thinking and feeling. Sharing relevant information means reducing that gap in a way that's productive. Here are several principles for deciding whether you are sharing all relevant information:

- Share information that doesn't support your view.
- Share information even if it might upset others.
- Share your feelings.
- Be timely in sharing information.
- Be transparent when you can't be transparent.

Share Information That Doesn't Support Your View

Sharing information that doesn't support your view ensures that everyone has a common pool of information, not just the information that favors your desired solution or purpose. If you want to outsource your division's IT support to save money but know that it will also reduce response time somewhat, that's relevant information to share. If you are planning to terminate a project that isn't generating adequate results and you know it will mean laying off some people, share that information clearly. By sharing information that doesn't support your view you build credibility and trust with those you work with.

Share Information Even If It Might Upset Others

Sometimes you have information that won't make people feel good—but you still need to share it. Giving team members negative feedback about their performance is a common example. Although you don't want to upset people, you also don't want to withhold relevant information just because sharing it might distress them. Withholding information may seem compassionate, but it usually has the opposite effect. If you withhold or downplay the feedback, you prevent people from getting the information they need to make an informed choice about changing their behavior. As a result, they're less likely to change, you will continue to be frustrated when they don't, and they will sense that you're concerned about something even if they can't identify what it is. You'll probably think to yourself, "What don't they understand, why are they not changing?" without real-

Withholding information may seem compassionate, but it usually has the opposite effect.

izing that you haven't clearly shared the feedback about what and why they need to change. By sharing the information you increase the chance for change.

Share Your Feelings

We all have feelings; there's no getting away from it. The challenge is to become aware of your feelings and to use them productively. If you try to bury them or understate them, they will fester and seep out, straining your relationships. If you simply act on them, you may find yourself blowing up, also damaging relationships. As Aristotle wrote in the *Nicomachean Ethics*, "Getting angry is easy. But to get angry with the right person, in the right way, for the right reasons . . . that is not easy."

Sharing your feelings helps others understand your views. If you're concerned about how someone might respond to your feed-back, say something like, "I want to share some feedback with you, and because you said you were annoyed with me last time I did so, I'm concerned that this may be difficult to hear." If you're interdependent with team members who aren't meeting agreed-upon deadlines, say something like, "I'm feeling really frustrated. We had agreed on these deadlines so I could meet my commitments to our customer. Now I can't make good on my commitment." When you share your feelings, include what has happened that leads you to feel the way you do. This enables others to decide for themselves whether the situation occurred as you stated it and make their own assessment about whether your reactions seem appropriate.

Be Timely in Sharing Information

Information is like food that comes packaged with a label "best if used by (date)." The longer you wait to share the relevant information, the less digestible it becomes. The research on feedback is clear: people are better able to remember and respond to feedback if it is given soon after the behavior. If you have negative information to share, don't wait until you have some positive feedback to give as well. Share the information as you get it.

Be Transparent When You Can't Be Transparent

Sometimes you have information that would be relevant to your coworkers, but you can't share it. The information may be proprietary, financial, protected by privacy laws, or involve other legal matters. In these situations you can be transparent about the fact that you can't be fully transparent.

Rather than let your team continue to address the issue without understanding that you're withholding certain information, tell them that you have relevant information that you're not able to share or can't share at this time. This allows the team and you to decide whether to delay making a decision or to accept your recommendation for a decision, recognizing that it is based partly on information they don't have access to.

If you can't share the relevant information because it comes from a source who asked that you keep it confidential, you can share this with the team. Then you can decide whether to go back to the person whose confidence you honored and ask under what conditions you can share it with your team, so that your team can make a more informed decision.

Being transparent about the fact you can't be fully transparent builds trust. It also helps maintain commitment to a decision, which might otherwise falter when people later learn the information that you were unable to share at the time.

BEHAVIOR 3: USE SPECIFIC EXAMPLES AND AGREE ON WHAT IMPORTANT WORDS MEAN

If you're trying to develop a common understanding in your team, you need to make sure that everyone is using the same words to mean the same thing. This sounds obvious, but in practice it is deceptively challenging. Two related ways to accomplish this are using specific examples and agreeing on what important words mean.

Name Names

I often call Behavior 3 the "name names" behavior. The more specific you are, the more likely people will understand, and that does include names of people. Sometimes you may be intentionally vague, saying something like, "Some of you haven't met your report deadlines this month. I still need your reports." You may hesitate to name names because you don't want to put people on the spot or embarrass them. But this kind of reasoning is often based on the assumption that identifying people by name in a team setting is necessarily embarrassing—and that assumption undermines the kind of accountability leaders say they want.

I return to that point in Chapter Six, but for now, it's enough to point out that when you're not specific, you can create the very problems you are trying to avoid: unnecessary misunderstanding, conflict, and defensiveness. When you don't name who "some of you" are, team members have to guess who you're talking about. People who haven't met the deadlines may think you understand their excuses and aren't talking about them, and people who have met the deadlines may think you've mislaid their reports and get defensive.

Instead of saying, "Some of you haven't met your report deadlines this month. I still need your reports," you can say, "Eric, Marija, and Peter, I didn't get a monthly report from you yet; did you send it?" By naming people, you make it clear who you are talking to. By asking whether they sent their reports, you're checking to see if they followed through—and testing your inference that if you didn't get them, they didn't send them. There are, after all, other reasons for a report to be missing from your inbox.

Ask What You Really Want to Know

Another form of naming names is saying specifically what you mean, without beating around the bush. I often hear leaders check to see whether others have accomplished a task by asking, "Did you get a chance to . . . ?"

I used to ask this question too, until a group of police chiefs broke me of the habit. I was helping the group learn how to manage conflict and started by asking, "How many of you had a chance to read the article that I asked you to read?" To my pleasant surprise, all fifty hands went up. "That's impressive," I said. "This is the first group I've worked with where everyone has read the article." One of the police chiefs spoke up. "Roger, you didn't ask us if we read the article; you asked us if we had a chance to read it. We all had a chance." "You're right," I said. "Let me try this again. How many of you read the assignment?" This time only about one-third of the chiefs raised their hands. In that encounter I realized I had asked "Did you have a chance to . . ." because I was trying to save face for those people who might not have completed the assignment. But, in doing so, I wasn't asking what I really meant and I wasn't asking people to be accountable.

Using this behavior, like all the behaviors, involves changing how you think. Instead of thinking that by identifying people, you're putting them on the spot, try thinking about this as being transparent, accountable, curious, and compassionate. With this new mindset you're giving people an opportunity to address your concerns, including whether they view the situation in the same way.

Use Examples to Agree on What Important Words Mean

At the heart of developing common understanding is making sure everyone is using a given word to mean the same thing. Sometimes the words that teams use most often are the ones that members define differently.

I worked with a group of elected and appointed officials responsible for developing a regional recycling plan. Less than an hour into the meeting, the group was making little progress, even on what seemed to be simple issues. I told the group that I thought they might be getting stuck because they had different definitions of what the word *co-mingled* meant. I asked each of them to give me an example of what a "co-mingled recycling box" would contain at the curb. One official said co-mingled recycling would mean that all paper, plastics, and bottles would be in one box. Another official said that paper, plastics, and bottles would be in three separate boxes but not otherwise sorted. A third official said that co-mingled meant that that brown, green, and clear bottles would be in separate boxes. After the group settled on a common definition, they were able to make progress on issues they hadn't managed to address, and they understood what their differences of opinion were.

If your definition of consensus is that most of the people on your team agree, but your team members' definition is that everyone on the team agrees, you're going to have a problem making decisions by consensus when only most of the people agree. If your definition of people getting on board is that they buy in to a solution that you have already developed, but their definition is that they jointly develop a solution with you, you'll be thinking that people are resisting getting on board when they are simply doing what they think *is* getting on board.

The solution is mechanically simple. When you use a word that you think others may define differently, define it by giving an example that includes specific behaviors. You might say something along these lines:

"My expectation is that all of you will hold each other accountable for each other's businesses. By *accountable*, I mean, for example, that when you hear someone say something about their business that you think may not make sense, you call attention to that with the person in the meeting. It's not an insult; you can't be any help if you don't understand what's happening, and building real understanding will ensure that we're working as a team to support each other. If someone makes a commitment to do something by a certain time that affects you or the team and you think they haven't met their commitment, raise the issue with them in the meeting. Does anyone have a different or additional view of holding each other accountable?"

If you hear someone using a word or term that you think there isn't clear agreement on, ask them to give an example. Say something like, "Perry, you said, 'We're not really acting like a team.' Can you give us a couple of examples of times when we didn't act like a team and say exactly what we would have done in those cases if we had acted like a team?" Asking people to "tell me about a time when" or "tell me a story about" is an easy way for people to give examples that are rich in detail.

BEHAVIOR 4: EXPLAIN REASONING AND INTENT

As I said in Chapter One, people are hardwired to make meaning. When you say, ask, or do something, others immediately try to figure out what you really mean. They ask themselves, "What's behind that statement? How did that conclusion come up?" Naturally, this is true especially for people over whom you have authority and power.

Explaining your reasoning and intent helps people understand what led you to make the comments you made, ask the questions you asked, or take the actions you took. It provides the information for others to understand how they should carry out your tasks, respond to your requests, and even understand how you would like them to think about issues.

I found out the downside of not explaining my reasoning and intent many years ago. I asked my administrative assistant, "Did you already mail the materials to Jeff Solana that I asked you to mail this morning?" As she was answering, "Yes," I added, "I'm asking because I need to correct some figures I included in the report." With that she responded, "Well, it's in my outbox, but I can redo it." Before I explained my intent, it's likely that my assistant incorrectly inferred that my question was designed to assess her performance. With that mindset, her answer "yes" was appropriate and accurate. But after I explained my intent, her interpretation of my question shifted to a request for her help, which was my real intent. Had I not explained my reasoning and intent, the letter would have been mailed with errors. This kind of missed opportunity occurs on a much larger scale every day in teams.

When you share your reasoning and intent, you reduce the need for others to figure out reasons why you are saying what you're saying. Without your explanation, people make up their own stories. Often the stories they tell themselves aren't accurate, and often they are negative, and almost always they feel just like facts to their creators.

Explaining your reasoning and intent can be as simple as adding, "I'm saying this (or doing this or asking this) because. . . ."

> *When you share your reasoning and intent, you reduce the need for others to figure out reasons why you are saying what you're saying.*

The Transparency Test

The time when leaders most consistently fail to explain their reasoning and intent is when they are describing the strategy they plan to follow in conducting a meeting. Notice I'm not talking about explaining their strategy for the business; I'm talking about explaining the strategy that they're using as they conduct the conversation or meeting.

In every meeting, you have a strategy for holding the conversation, though many times you're not conscious of the strategy or even that you're using one. The strategy includes the steps you'll take so the meeting will follow the process you want so you can achieve your desired outcome. Just as you have a strategy for the meeting, so do others in the meeting. If your strategies differ, you'll quickly realize that people want to take the conversation in directions you don't want to go and you'll begin to worry that you won't get the outcomes you want. The strategy or process for the meeting is important because if people are using unilateral strategies, whoever controls the meeting strategy largely influences the outcome. This leads people to fight for control over the meeting process, but the fight is rarely overt.

Sometimes you're not transparent about your strategy for the conversation because you want to hide it. This happens when you're trying to unilaterally control the conversation to achieve your desired outcome or trying to minimize the expression of negative feelings—or both. The sandwich approach to feedback is a really good example of this, as I mentioned in Chapter One. Many leaders are taught to use the sandwich approach to feedback when they have some negative feedback to give. They start and end with positive feedback, "sandwiching" the negative feedback in the middle.

But it's useful to think about the reasoning underlying this strategy. Do you remember what the person who taught it to you said? It was probably something like this:

> "Starting off on a positive note makes the person more comfortable so it's easier to hear the negative feedback without getting defensive; ending on a positive note maintains the person's self-esteem and reduces the person's anger, which makes the session less likely to blow up in your face."

Here's a simple and powerful three-step thought experiment to help you figure out if you're about to use a unilaterally controlling strategy. I call it the transparency test:

1. *Identify the strategy you're using to have the conversation.* In the sandwich approach, the strategy is when you have negative feedback to give someone, start off on a positive note to make the person more comfortable and make it easier to hear your negative feedback without getting defensive. Next, give the negative feedback, which is the reason you wanted to talk. Finally, give some more positive feedback, so the person will leave the meeting with self-esteem in place and won't be as angry with you.

2. *Imagine explaining your strategy to the ones you are using it with.* Also imagine asking them whether the strategy will work for them: "Lee, I called you in here to give you some negative feedback and I want to let you know my strategy for having the conversation and see if it will work for you. First, I'm going to give you some positive feedback to make you feel more comfortable and get you ready for the negative feedback, because I think you're going to get defensive. Then, I'll give you the negative feedback, which is why I called you in here today. Finally, I'll give you some more positive feedback so you'll feel better about yourself and won't be as angry with me. Will that work for you, Lee?"

> *The solution here isn't simply being transparent about your unilaterally controlling strategy; it's shifting your mindset so you begin using mutual learning strategies that become more effective when you share them with others.*

3. *Notice your reaction.* If you find yourself laughing at the absurdity of what you're thinking, or if you're thinking *"I could never share* that *strategy,"* you've probably identified a unilateral control strategy that keeps you from being transparent. You keep your unilateral control strategies private because they work only when others don't know what you're doing or when they agree to play along.

The solution here isn't simply being transparent about your uni-laterally controlling strategy; it's shifting your mindset so you begin using mutual learning strategies that become more effective when you share them with others.

Don't Bury the Lead

Good journalists know not to "bury the lead"—the main point of a news story, which should be stated in the first sentence or two. A good lead helps the reader quickly understand what the story is about and where it's heading. This principle is also essential in working together as a team.

Take a situation in which you're concerned that a direct report is not meeting deadlines, which is causing you additional work. A good lead would be, "Frank, I want to talk with you about deadlines that I think you've been missing during the last month and how it is causing me additional work. Is this a good time to talk?" Simple, right?

But when I observe leaders in action, few of them naturally begin such conversations that way. Instead they usually have eased into it. Here are several examples of how they would start:

- "Frank, how do you think your work is going?"
- "Frank, there are some things I want us to go over, and maybe you and I could explore them a bit."
- "Frank, do you have a few minutes? I need to talk to you about some of your behavior that is concerning me."

In the first example, you hope that Frank will tell you what you need to tell him, so you won't have to say it. In the meantime, Frank is wondering why you're asking. The second example is so vague that Frank has no idea where you're headed. The third example is a little less vague but also ominous. Not only will Frank have no idea what kind of behavior you're talking about, but the phrase "your behavior" is likely to start Frank worrying about all the terrible possibilities that might exist. All three examples create anxiety for Frank.

Why do we bury the lead? Because we're reluctant to say what we're really thinking. It's uncomfortable for us to talk about and we assume it will be uncomfortable for the other party, too. Ironically, by burying the lead, you increase the discomfort for yourself and others, rather than reduce it. The longer you bury the lead, the more the discomfort and anxiety rises, for you and others. You get increasingly anxious about what you need to say and haven't said yet. Others get increasingly anxious wondering what you are hiding. The sooner you share your lead, the sooner the anxiety decreases and the more time you have to address the problem.

Start with the lead. If you're starting a meeting, in the first two sentences tell others what you want to talk about and why. The more specific you can be the better. "Frank, I'd like to talk with you about the deadlines for the Livingston project that I think you've been missing during the last month and how playing catch-up is causing me additional work. I think it will take about thirty minutes. Do you have time to talk now?"

HALF-WAY THERE

Here is a quick summary of the four mutual learning behaviors covered so far:

1. State views and ask genuine questions.
   - Raise your curiosity, don't lower your passion.
   - Make sure your questions are genuine.
   - Try adding "you idiot" to a question to see whether it is rhetorical.
   - Open your gifts.
   - Remember that curiosity doesn't mean agreement.
2. Share all relevant information.
   - Share information that doesn't support your view.
   - Share information even if it might upset others.
   - Share your feelings.

- Be timely in sharing information.
- Be transparent when you can't be transparent.

3. Use specific examples and agree on what important words mean.
   - Name names.
   - Ask what you really want to know.
   - Use examples to make sure everyone sees what important words mean.

4. Explain reasoning and intent.
   - Be transparent about meeting strategy.
   - Don't bury the lead.

CHAPTER 5

Putting the Puzzle Together
Mutual Learning Behaviors 5–8

This chapter continues with four more behaviors that stem from the mutual learning mindset—those highlighted in Figure 5.1.

BEHAVIOR 5: FOCUS ON INTERESTS, NOT POSITIONS[1]

Have you ever been in a meeting where people try unsuccessfully to get others to buy in to their solutions? The first person shares a solution and the others all say why it won't work. Then the second person speaks and that idea is likewise shot down. The team eventually reaches an impasse or agrees on a compromise that pleases no one, or the leader takes the decision away from the team.

Why does this happen? First, people are natural problem solvers. Give a group a problem, and the members will quickly generate solutions for it. They come to the meeting with solutions already in hand, or they quickly come up with them. Second, when people have strong feelings about the topic, they think of the meeting as

Behavior

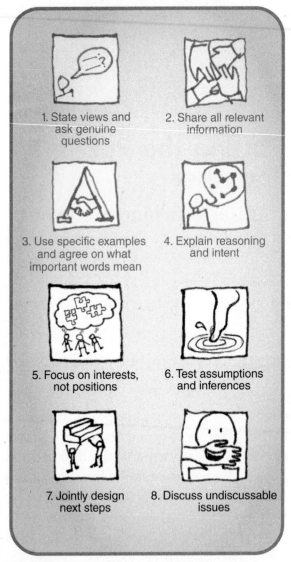

1. State views and ask genuine questions

2. Share all relevant information

3. Use specific examples and agree on what important words mean

4. Explain reasoning and intent

5. Focus on interests, not positions

6. Test assumptions and inferences

7. Jointly design next steps

8. Discuss undiscussable issues

Figure 5.1. Behaviors Discussed in This Chapter

Source: Roger Schwarz & Associates; used with permission.

a contest where their view—which they see as the correct one—should prevail. That leads them to try to convince others that their solution is the right one. But that doesn't explain why one person's solution is often unacceptable to others. To understand this, you need to understand how people arrive at preferred solutions. Basically, we generate a solution that meets *our* needs and concerns, because those are what we know about. When our solutions don't take into account other team members' needs and concerns, the team rejects them.

Think of positions as the solutions that people identify to address an issue. In contrast, think of interests as the underlying needs that people use to generate their positions. To illustrate, if you and I are sitting in a conference room, and I want the window open and you want it closed, those are our positions.[2] If I asked you, "What leads you to want the window closed?" you might say that the wind is blowing your papers around and you want them together. If you asked what leads me to want the window open, I might say that I'm warm and I want to be cooler. These are our interests. My solution to open the window and your solution to shut it are simply ways for each of us to meet our interests. The problem here is that the window can't be open and closed at the same time. But if we focus on our interests, we can probably find a solution that meets both sets of interests.

As my example suggests, the difficulty with solving problems by focusing first on positions is that people's positions are often in conflict, even when their interests are compatible. This happens because people tend to offer positions that meet their own interests but do not take into account other people's interests. In the example, you would probably reject my initial solution, and I would probably reject yours, because neither met the other's interests.

Four Steps to Building Commitment

Leaders often ask me how to get commitment from their team. The answer is simple. *People commit to decisions that meet their interests.*

If you understand and craft a solution that addresses their interests, team members will naturally commit.

Focusing on interests makes it possible to identify these interests and then ask the question, "How can we solve this problem in a way that meets both of our interests?" In the window example, with a little thought and creativity, we might decide to open the top part of the window so that your papers were not being blown by the wind and I still got the benefit of cool air. Or we could switch places so that I was closer to the open window and you were away from it. When we focus on interests, we are being transparent by explaining the reasoning and intent underlying our preferences, and we are being curious by learning about others' interests.

People commit to decisions that meet their interests.

Here are four steps for building commitment by focusing on interests:

Step 1: *Identify interests.* Ask team members to complete this sentence as many times as possible: "Regardless of the specifics of any solution we develop, it needs to be one that . . ." In that way, build a single list of interests. As people keep identifying positions, ask them, "What is it about your solution that's important to you?" This helps identify their underlying interests.

Step 2: *Agree on interests to consider in the solution.* In this step the team clarifies what each interest means and reaches agreement on which interests they'll consider in developing solutions. One way to ask this question is "Are there any interests that someone thinks we should not take into account when developing a solution?" "Take into account" doesn't mean that everyone agrees that a given interest is important, just that everyone sees it as relevant. In the end the team won't necessarily be able to craft a solution that meets all the relevant interests, though that would be the ideal outcome. At the end of this step, your team will have a single list of the interests that an ideal solution would address.

Step 3: *Craft solutions that meet the interests.* Now your team is ready to generate solutions that meet as many of the interests as possible—ideally all of them. At this step you can say something like, "Let's come up with some possible solutions that meet all our interests. We're not committing to any of these solutions yet, we're just getting them on the table." The group begins to identify possible solutions. This is a time for members to play off and build on each other's ideas, seeking solutions that incorporate as many interests as possible. If you can't find a solution that meets the agreed-upon interests, consider whether all the proposed solutions have a common unnecessary assumption embedded in them. For example, if every proposed solution assumes that the work has to be performed only by full-time employees, try relaxing that assumption and see if the team can generate other solutions that will meet all the interests. If this does not help, then the team can prioritize or weight the different interests to find a solution that addresses the most important ones.

Step 4: *Select a solution and implement it.* Using this approach doesn't guarantee that the team will reach a decision that meets everyone's interests. It does, however, increase the chance that you will find a solution that everyone can support.

When Owen Grant worked with Phil Hughes to build broader support for the early pay discount program, Owen was focusing on interests, not positions. At the beginning of the conversation, Owen knew only Phil's position—that he didn't want the early pay program. Only when Owen got curious and asked for Phil's reasoning did he learn that Phil's main interest was saving money, which he believed the company would do more effectively by timing payments than by taking what he regarded as insignificant discounts. Owen was able to show Phil how the early pay discount program would still meet Phil's interest. Had the program not met Phil's interest, then the two of them could have jointly explored how to modify the program so it did.

Why Listing Pros and Cons Doesn't Work

Many teams develop a list of pros and cons to compare potential solutions. But when you ask your team to develop a list of pros and cons for specific solutions, you're reinforcing team members' *positions.* Team members quickly realize that the winning solution will be the one with the longest list of pros and the shortest list of cons. So they identify as many pros as possible for their own solution and as many cons as possible for others' solutions, and problem solving deteriorates into a competition.

When you ask people to focus on *interests*, the dynamics change. When the team is trying to craft solutions, members have little motivation to push solutions that meet only their interests. If the team can't identify a solution that meets all the interests they have agreed on, the entire team finds itself stuck in the same boat, rather than getting annoyed at people who have an opposing solution. Psychologically, focusing on interests leads the team to pull together; focusing on pros and cons can easily pull it apart.

"Don't Come With a Problem Unless You Have a Solution"

In some teams, people are expected not to raise a problem unless they have a solution in mind. On the surface this policy makes sense, but it can create more problems. You want your team members to take initiative and accountability for solving problems rather than just presenting them to you or the team to solve. And you want to reduce the time you need to spend in meetings; they're difficult to schedule and consume valuable team time. But it's presumptuous to expect that a solution will work for everyone without knowing their differing interests.

If you're not careful, asking team members to come to the team with a solution can take more time rather than less because, once again, it reinforces a focus on positions. They'll come to the meeting with a solution based on the interests they have access to—their own. As soon as they present their solution, team members will challenge it if it doesn't meet their interests. Soon team members are arguing over positions as each person tosses in a personally satisfactory solution, wasting time and damaging relationships. This scenario is predictable and preventable.

Instead, before someone comes to the team with a proposed solution, ask that team member to learn and understand the other team members' interests in the matter and to propose a solution that meets these interests. That means that before the meeting, the team member will need to find out the others' interests, saying things like, "I'm trying to address the issue of X and want to propose a solution to the team that will meet everyone's needs. So, can you tell me what needs have to be met in any solution I develop?"

At the team meeting, the member with the proposal can say something like, "I've talked with each of you about the interests that need to be met to solve X. I think I've got a solution that works for all of us. Let me lay out the solution and describe how I think it meets each of the interests you mentioned. Then let's find out if I missed anything." Requiring this approach lets you save team time and still focus on interests.

My colleagues and I worked with a local government after it had been trying unsuccessfully for over a year to merge its public works and engineering departments. The various stakeholders had focused on their positions—such as who would control a newly merged department—and failed to develop a plan. In a series of meetings, we brought the relevant stakeholders into a room, identified the different interests that needed to be met, and then asked subgroups to propose solutions that met the interests. The group explored the different solutions and then crafted a final plan that integrated parts of the different solutions to best meet the interests they had identified. The plan was accepted and successfully implemented in less than three months and has now functioned successfully for more than four years.

BEHAVIOR 6: TEST ASSUMPTIONS AND INFERENCES

Human beings are hardwired to make meaning out of events. When you hear people say things or see them do things, or you get e-mail from them, you try to figure out, "What's this person really saying? Why are they really doing this?"

For example, suppose Hank's manager Jim says, "Your team's been doing a great job, but the project has been slowing your team down. I'm going to give Donna's group the project to manage." Immediately Hank may wonder, *What does Jim really mean when he says that? Why is he saying that?* Then he attempts to answer his own questions by telling himself a story. He might tell himself that Jim is concerned about his team's performance and isn't telling the complete truth. Or he may think that Jim is shifting the work because he won't confront Donna about the unreliable cost projections she is providing Hank to use in the project, which is why his team is behind. Hank is probably not aware that he's asking and answering these questions in his mind. But he'll use the story he tells himself as he responds to the situation. If this story is a negative one, he'll respond in a negative way. For example, he might say sarcastically, "Thanks a lot," or simply, "You're making a big mistake."

Don't Believe Everything You Think

The problem isn't that people tell themselves stories about what's happening; the problem is that they automatically believe them. When you draw a conclusion about things you don't know based on things you do know, you're making an inference. When you simply take something for granted, without any information, you're making an assumption. You naturally make inferences and assumptions all the time: you must, to get through the day. And you can't test out every inference you make; if you did, you would drive people crazy and you wouldn't get anything done. Still, the problem is that when you make inferences, you don't know whether they are correct. And if you act on your inferences as if they are true when they are false, you create problems for yourself and others. The only way you can determine if your inference is accurate is to test it with the person or people you're making the inference about. That's what this behavior does.

To decide whether to test your inference, ask yourself, "What are the consequences of acting as if my inference is true if it is in fact untrue?" If you decide the risk of not testing your inference is too high, then test it. Testing an inference has three parts. First you become aware of the assumptions and inferences you're making. Second, you convert a risky inference into a form you can test. Third, you test whether that view is accurate before you act on it.

How You Tell Yourself Stories: The Ladder of Inference

How you tell yourself these stories is called the ladder of inference (See Figure 5.2).[3] Let's take the example I introduced earlier, where Hank's boss gives Donna the project to manage. What Jim just said to Hank is what we call observable information. *Observable information* is anything you can record on a video camera; this includes what people say, their nonverbal expressions, things they write, e-mail they send, reports, spreadsheets, and PowerPoint presentations. Of course, someone working for Jim will have other observable information from him, including what he has said in the past about the person's own work, Donna's work, and so on.

The first step you take up the ladder is to select some of the observable information to make sense out of. Even a face-to-face conversation has too much verbal and nonverbal information for your brain to capture it all, so you focus on certain elements and forget about others. If you're Hank, and concerned about losing part of your work, you might hear only the part where Jim said, "The project has been slowing your group down. I'm giving Donna's group the project to manage." You may have missed the part where Jim says, "Your team's been doing a great job."

You take the second step up the ladder when you react to and try to make meaning of the observable information you've selected. Your reaction may be *I'm angry*. As you think about what it means, you think *He's saying we haven't done our job well and he is taking away part of my job permanently*. Next you begin to ask yourself why

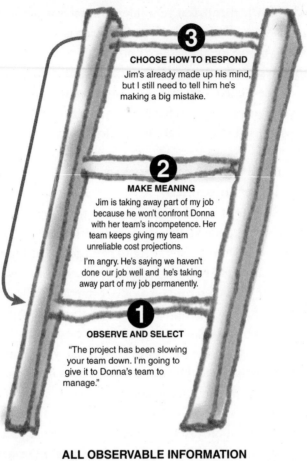

ALL OBSERVABLE INFORMATION
"Hank, your team's been doing a great job, but the project has been slowing your team down. I'm going to give it to Donna's team to manage."

Figure 5.2. The Ladder of Inference

Source: Roger Schwarz & Associates; used with permission.

this happened. You might think *Jim is taking away part of my job because he won't confront Donna with her team's incompetence. Her team keeps giving my team unreliable projections. We're getting blamed for her mistakes.* When you reach conclusions about why people are doing what they are doing, you're making a special kind of inference called an *attribution*. Attributions are simply motives we assign to people. In this case, Hank attributes to Jim a fear of confronting Donna.

Notice the inferences that Hank made—the conclusions he reached based on Jim's words. Jim never said that Hank wasn't doing his job well. Jim never said that he was taking away part of Hank's job permanently. Jim never said he was concerned about confronting Donna about her team's incompetence. And Jim never said that he was blaming Hank for Donna's team's incompetence. All of these are inferences that Hank made and that he will soon act on as if they are true—unless he's careful to check them out.

Finally, at the third step on the ladder of inference you decide how to respond, based on the story you told yourself. Hank might think *Jim has already made up his mind, but I still need to tell him he's making a big mistake*. Before he realizes that he's reacting to himself and not to Jim, he blurts out, "Thanks a lot" or "You're making a big mistake."

This kind of reaction is a natural human instinct. We all do it a lot of the time. What makes these situations so challenging is that you climb the ladder of inference quickly without realizing you're doing it. Most of the time, you're simply not aware when you've left the realm of directly observable information and started making inferences. So the challenge is to become aware.

When you make an inference and assume it's true, you reinforce your inference. As the arrow in Figure 5.2 illustrates, the inference you make leads you to look for information that confirms your inference and ignore information that disconfirms it. Because many of the situations you face can be interpreted in more than one way, it's easy to interpret situations so they confirm your initial inference. It's through this process that you convert your initial inferences into what feel like real facts without ever testing whether they are true.

Becoming Aware of Your Ladder of Inference

To see if you're making an inference, ask yourself this simple but powerful question: "Did the person say or write those words exactly? If not, what exact words differ from how I'm thinking about it?"

When you identify the gap between what the person said and the conclusions you've drawn, you have identified the inferences you made.

Identifying this gap is challenging work. You need to listen carefully to what others are saying so that you can accurately remember the key words and not change them. You also need to monitor your own thought process. The more you practice this, the easier it gets.

Keep in mind that just because you've make an attribution or other inference, that doesn't mean it's incorrect, either. It simply means you can't know whether it's accurate without asking the person in question. That's the purpose of the behavior—to make sure you're making an informed choice before you act on information that may not be accurate.

Lowering Your Ladder: Making Your Inferences Testable

Sometimes the inferences you make are far removed from the data you used to make them. I call these high-level inferences. Hank's attribution that Jim is taking away part of his job permanently because he's afraid to confront Donna with her team's incompetence is a high-level inference. To reach that conclusion correctly, Hank had to make a number of other inferences that must all be true.

Making higher-level inferences creates the same problem as climbing higher on a real ladder—it gets riskier the higher you climb. High-level inferences are more challenging to test out because they easily make people defensive. If you're Hank inferring that Jim is taking away part of your job because he's afraid of Donna, you may end up saying something like, "Are you afraid of Donna?" or worse, "Are you a coward?" Neither one of those questions is likely to lead to a helpful response from Jim. He's likely to feel insulted and shut down or worse. What you need is a way of lowering the ladder of inference so as to stay closer to the data, which also makes it easier to test inferences. Figure 5.3 shows the difference between making a high-level inference and a low-level inference.

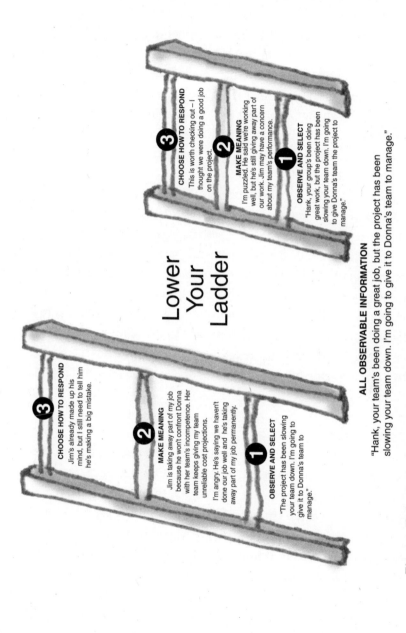

Figure 5.3. Lowering Your Ladder of Inference

Source: Roger Schwarz and Associates; used with permission.

The first step in lowering your ladder is to ask yourself, "What did the person say and do that leads me to believe this inference I'm making?" When you ask yourself this question, you naturally take yourself down to the bottom of the ladder where the observable information is. Now you can jog your memory and see if what you initially thought you heard is what might have been said. Did Jim really say he was taking away part of the job permanently or did he just say he was giving the project to Donna's team to manage without saying how long this would last? This step isn't foolproof, but it requires you to become more rigorous about identifying the observable information.

The second step is to ask yourself, "What explanation is closer to the data and more generous?" In other words, "What inference can I make that isn't so high level and has some generosity of spirit?" In the Jim-Hank example, Hank might infer that Jim does have some concerns about Hank's performance, because Jim said, "The project has been slowing you down." This is a lower-level inference than inferring that Jim is afraid of confronting Donna with her team's incompetence. It also is generous in spirit toward Jim; it starts from a basic assumption that Jim is acting with good will toward Hank, even if he isn't being fully transparent. This generosity of spirit is part of compassion.

Testing Your Inference

After you have generated a generous inference that is close to the observable data, you are ready to test out your inference. Start by stating the observable behavior that led you to make your inference and ask if you have the correct information. Hank might say something like, "Jim, a minute ago I think you said that 'the project has been slowing your team down' and that you're 'going to give it to Donna's team to manage.' Did I hear that right?" Assuming Jim says that's correct, Hank would move to the second step and test the inference by saying something like, "That made me think that you have some concerns about how we're handling the project. Am I off base at all?" At this point, Jim might say, "No, I don't have any concerns about your team's performance. I know it's not your fault that Donna's team is giving your team bad projections." Or Jim might say, "Well, now that you've mentioned it, I do have some concern." Whatever Jim's response, Hank has tested the inference. And by continuing to be curious, he can learn more.

When you use this behavior, you apply transparency and accountability to your thinking and reveal a curiosity about what others think.

Testing Inferences in a Team

While you speak in your team meetings, each of your direct reports is privately telling a story about what you really mean. After people leave a team meeting they may gather informally, trying to figure out what you really meant and why you said what you said. Unfortunately, the members test their inferences about you by getting together and asking *each other* what they think *you* meant. Then together they try to create some common story that makes sense to them. The problem? You are the only person who really knows what you meant.

This happened when I was working with an organization's top HR leader and his HR team. The conversation went something like this with a team member I'll call Gwen:

Gwen: Mark is always trying to rush me out of his office before we're finished with our meeting.

Roger: What exactly does he do that leads you to think that?

Gwen: Every time I say something, he taps his pencil on his desk and says, "uh-huh, uh-huh."

Roger: And have you checked out your inference?

Gwen: Sure, I've checked it out with everyone.

Roger: Who is everyone?

Gwen: Everyone on the team. [She mentions the team members' names and each of them confirms that Mark does the same thing in meetings with them.]

Roger: Have any of you checked your inference with Mark?

Team Members: No.

Roger: How about checking it out now?

Gwen: So, Mark, when you tap your pencil and keep on saying "uh-huh," are you trying to end the meeting?

Mark: Not at all. That's just my way of mentally keeping track of what you're saying. It's my way of saying, "I understand, go on." I was wondering why all of you were leaving my meetings before they were over.

This simple but common story carries two lessons. First, you need to test your inference with the person about whom you're making it. Although it may seem easier to test out your inference with others who are in a situation similar to yours, all these people are simply posing their own equally unverified inferences.

Second, if you make an inference about something a teammate said or did in a team setting and it's relevant to other team members, ultimately you need to clarify the inference in the team setting so everyone has a common understanding of what that teammate meant. Without this, team members will continue to act on their incorrect inferences. If Gwen had tested her inference privately with Mark and they never shared their conversation with the entire team, they wouldn't be acting accountably toward the team, they would be preventing the team from making an informed choice, and everyone else on the team would continue to interact with Mark continuing to believe that he was trying to shut down meetings with them. This is

> *If team members learned nothing more about mutual learning than the need to test out their inferences firsthand, they would make huge improvements in the results they get and the relationships they build.*

what distinguishes accountability to your boss or direct report from accountability to your team.

In my experience, untested inferences are among the main reasons that teams get stuck. If team members learned nothing more about mutual learning than the need to test out their inferences firsthand, they would make huge improvements in the results they get and the relationships they build. Testing inferences also improves your mental health. You spend much less time worried or frustrated about what others may be thinking. Instead you find out, so you and others can use your time more productively.

BEHAVIOR 7: JOINTLY DESIGN NEXT STEPS

When you jointly design next steps, you design them with others instead of for others. Joint design is a way to be transparent and curious, and to enable others to make informed choices. It increases the chance that you will get a genuinely workable solution and that people will be committed to implementing it.

Want to know what it feels like when you don't get to jointly design next steps? Think about a meeting you attended that was really important to you when the person running the meeting set the agenda, decided who talked and for how long, and determined what information members could share and what information was not relevant. If your views differed from the meeting leader's views, you probably quickly realized that you wouldn't influence the outcome because you couldn't influence the unilateral process. You probably felt that decisions weren't as good as they could have been because not everyone got to share their relevant information. As a result, there was little commitment to follow through with these decisions. Now imagine how others react when you unilaterally control a meeting or conversation.

You can jointly design any next steps. For example, consider beginning meetings, keeping the meeting on track, and resolving disagreements—all high-leverage situations to use joint design.

Beginning Meetings: Purpose Before Process Before Content

When you begin a meeting using joint design you agree on the purpose of the meeting, then agree on the process for the meeting, before starting into the meeting content.

Agree on the Meeting Purpose

If it's your meeting, let people know in your first two sentences what your purpose is for the meeting. The purpose isn't the topic and it's not the agenda. It's the reason you're discussing the topic and going through the agenda. By having agreement on the purpose, everyone knows why they are present and how to contribute. "This quarter we've had major unforecast declines in revenue. The purpose of this meeting is develop a plan for identifying the root causes so we can reverse this trend." After you've stated your purpose, check to see if others have a different understanding or believe other topics need to be added. "Does anyone have a different understanding of the purpose? Are there any other topics we need to address in order to address this issue?"

Agree on the Meeting Process

Next reach agreement on the process the team will use to move through the meeting. Without an agreed-upon agenda and process, everyone follows their own. Members naturally and reasonably take the meeting down a track that makes sense to them. But since members have different ideas about what needs to be discussed, this almost guarantees that someone will think that someone else is off track. Of course, the meeting can't be off-track if your team hasn't agreed on what the track is.

To reach agreement on the agenda and process you might say something like, "Given the purpose, I proposed the following agenda, which I e-mailed each of you yesterday: Let's start by going around the room and identifying the revenue figures for each of the businesses. After we have agreement on the figures, let's move to data that you have about potential root causes. After that, we'll discuss what steps to take. Anyone want to suggest changes to the agenda? Anything I missed?" You don't have to lay out the entire process for the meeting if it's not clear what the process will be. Just reach agreement on the steps you are clear about.

Finally, before you dive into the meeting content, be clear about how the decisions will be made. If your team members think that they will be making the decision as a team and discover that you're making the decision, they may be surprised and frustrated. Say something like, "I'd like to reach consensus—that is, unanimous support—on our decision. We have two hours to discuss this before I need to get an answer to John. So, if we can't reach consensus by then, I'll make the decision using the information from our meeting. If I need to make the decision, I'll let you know what it is before we leave." Now you're ready to start discussing the first step of the process you agreed on.

Keeping the Meeting on Track

Sometimes you think a team member is off-topic. If you think Lauren is off-track, rather than unilaterally control the conversation by saying, "Let's get back on track" or "That's not what we're talking about today," try being more curious. Consider saying something like, "I don't see how your point about outsourcing is related to the topic of our planning process. Am I missing something? Can you help me understand how you see them related?"

When Lauren responds, you and other team members might learn about a connection between the two topics that you hadn't considered. For example, Lauren might say that outsourcing will free up internal resources so that the team can complete the planning process in less time. If there is a connection, the team can decide whether it makes more sense to explore Lauren's idea now or later. If it turns out that Lauren's comment is not related, you can suggest placing it on a future agenda, if it's relevant.

This isn't simply a nice way of dealing with people who really are off-track. It's a way to suspend your assumption that you understand the situation and others don't, to be curious about others' views, and to ask people to be accountable for their own contributions so that the team can make an informed choice about how best to move forward.

Resolving Disagreements Over Facts

When team members find themselves disagreeing with each other, typically they each try to convince the others that their own position is correct. The disagreement escalates as they each offer evidence to support their own position and skip over information that might weaken that position. In the end, the losers will still believe they are right.

But it's different when you jointly design a way to test a disagreement. Consider a conversation in which you and your team members disagree about whether proposed changes to your customer service will lead to increased or decreased costs. Together, you and the team would develop a way to figure out how the proposed changes could potentially increase or decrease costs and by how much. Jointly designing the test includes agreeing on what data to collect and what process to use in collecting it. Team members decide together who to consult, what questions to ask, what sources to use, and what statistical data to consider relevant. Whatever method you use, it's critical that the team members involved agree to it and agree about how to use the information gathered.

Experiment with Resolution

If you have an engineering or science background, you can think of jointly designing ways to test disagreements as an experiment. You're conducting an experiment with someone who has a competing hypothesis. But because you're jointly designing it, the two of you have to design the experimental method so it's rigorous enough to satisfy both of you. As long as that's the case, you can both agree to use the results, whatever they may be.

As with the other behaviors I recommend, to use joint design effectively, your mindset needs to be mutual learning. This means shifting from thinking that you are right and others who disagree are wrong to assuming that each of you may be missing something that the other sees. By jointly resolving disagreements, members make more informed choices, and they are more likely to commit to the outcome because they helped design the test and agreed to abide by its results.

The Squeaky Sofa

Here's an example from my personal life about jointly designing ways to test disagreements. I often find myself in consumer complaint situations: I'm the consumer and I'm complaining. In one of my classic customer complaint situations, I bought a sofa that squeaked. When I informed the store owner, he told me that my sofa was just like the other ones he sold. I suggested that we jointly design a way to see whether my sofa was just like the ones he sold. I proposed that we test three similar sofas in his warehouse and see if they squeaked and then we sit on my sofa to see if it squeaked. If mine squeaked and the others didn't, then we could conclude that mine was below their normal standard and I would get a new sofa for nothing. If the warehouse sofas also squeaked, then I'd have to pay more money if I wanted a sofa that didn't squeak. He agreed to the joint design and he and I met at the warehouse.

He had an assistant bring out three sofas—the same model and color that I had purchased. Both of us sat on the three sofas, bouncing up and down to see if they squeaked. None did. Then the store owner said, "Take this pen and make a small mark on one of these sofas in a place that's hard to see. This way if you get a new sofa, you'll get the one that you marked and we'll know it didn't squeak in the warehouse." Smart move. We were jointly trying to determine if the warehouse sofas were of the same quality as my sofa and he wanted to make sure that we were controlling for the important variable of location. If the sofa I marked squeaked at my house, we might conclude that it was my floor creating the problem, not the sofa.

When I suggested that the next step was for him to see if the sofa in my living room squeaked, he said, "I'll send an assistant to check it out." I said, "I don't think that will work; we sat on your sofas together; I think it's important that we check out my sofa together so we both have the same data firsthand." He agreed and showed up the next day with a truck, two assistants, and my marked sofa, just in case.

I showed the owner to the sofa and he sat down on it, moving from end to end gently bouncing up and down. He turned to his assistants and said, "This one squeaks. Bring in the other sofa. He gets it for nothing."

I asked the owner, "What do you think about the way we dealt with our disagreement?" His answer was telling. He didn't talk about who won and who lost. He said, "This was a really fair way to resolve our disagreement." He also told me it was the most educational consumer complaint he had ever been involved in.

As the owner left with my squeaky sofa, I sat in my new silent sofa. My wife, noticing me smile contently said, "You're really happy about this, aren't you?" "Yeah," I said, "This stuff isn't just theory—it really works."

The key here was that the owner and I jointly designed the process we would use to test our disagreement and we agreed—in advance—on what actions we would take depending on which sofas squeaked. You can use this process for any situation where you disagree on the facts and have some way of testing them out.

Degrees of Joint Design

You don't have to jointly design every next step. And when you jointly design a next step, you don't have to do it from scratch. In my sofa case, I didn't ask the owner how we should resolve our conflict; I proposed a design and then asked if it would work for him.

Sometimes you'll have a next step fully formed that you can present to others. In those situations, joint design begins with stating your proposed next step or solution and then asking, "What do you think about my proposed solution? Anything that you think I've missed?" The minimum requirement for joint design is that you genuinely ask for feedback on your proposal and then genuinely consider the feedback before making a decision.

At other times you won't have a next step ready to propose. Here joint design begins with saying something like, "I don't have any developed ideas about how we should proceed. How about if we talk about what makes sense?" At this point you and the team begin to explore the topic and jointly craft a next step from scratch.

There isn't one right way to jointly design next steps. The idea is to involve others early enough so that whoever is making the decision does so based on accurate assumptions and information and meets as many stakeholder interests as possible. In general, the more commitment you need, the more you want to involve the team and the more accountability you want to give them for having a role in the decision.

Keep in mind that joint design doesn't mean that you give up your prerogative of making the final decision. That right stems from your authority as the formal leader. Joint design identifies how early or late you bring your team into the problem-solving process to determine next steps. Regardless of when you bring your team into the process, the question remains how the decision will be made about what the next step will be. Will the decision require the team's consensus? Will you take a team vote? Will you make the final decision? Will you make the final decision only if the team can't reach consensus in a reasonable amount of time? These are all options for making the decision at the end of a joint design.

BEHAVIOR 8: DISCUSS UNDISCUSSABLE ISSUES

Essentially, this last behavior involves using the other seven in particularly challenging situations. Think about the last time you were walking to a meeting, complaining to a coworker about how the meeting was going to be a waste of time. You might be complaining that one team member is never prepared, or that one member dominates the conversation, or that everyone in the meeting acts as if they will meet the project deadline, when privately everyone knows they won't. In the meeting, the situation unfolds just as you predicted, but no one says anything, including you. Walking back to your office with your coworker, you again express your frustration about the team.

Does this sound familiar? If so, you're facing an undiscussable issue. Undiscussable issues are topics that are relevant to the team's work but that team members don't address in the team, the one place where they can be resolved. The undiscussable issue might involve the performance of one or more team members in which the quality, quantity, or timeliness of their work is having a negative impact on the team. That team member might be you as the leader. One study found that almost 50 percent of team members identified management practice—including their boss's leadership—as an undiscussable issue.[4] Or it might be about how the entire team is acting. I worked with a software leadership team in which the team routinely ran late releasing new versions of their software. Everyone on the team was aware of this and yet everyone acted as if it wasn't occurring. No one discussed the issue in front of the team, however much they complained about it in other places, such as one-on-one with those they trusted and agreed with.

Undiscussable issues are topics that are relevant to the team's work but that team members don't address in the team, the one place where they can be resolved.

People usually don't raise undiscussable issues because they're concerned that doing so will make some team members feel embarrassed or defensive. They try to save face for these team members— and for themselves as well. In short, they see discussing undiscussable issues as being uncompassionate. Another reason people don't like to raise undiscussable issues is that they think it will generate conflict, and they don't like conflict.

Unfortunately, many people overestimate the risk of raising an undiscussable issue and underestimate the risk of not raising it. Specifically, they overlook the negative systemic—and cruel—consequences they create by not raising undiscussable issues. Consider three team members—Heather, Carlos, and Stan—who are concerned about the poor performance of two other team members—Lynn and Jim—and how that performance affects the ability of the rest of the team to excel. If Heather, Carlos, and Stan don't raise this issue directly with Lynn and Jim, they will likely continue to talk about Lynn and Jim behind their backs. Lynn and Jim won't know what the others' concerns are, and so will be unable to make an informed choice about whether to change their behavior. Because Lynn and Jim aren't changing their behavior, Heather, Carlos, and Stan will continue to privately complain about them while simultaneously withholding the very information that could change the situation. Further, Heather, Carlos, and Stan will probably be unaware that they, too, are contributing to the problem by not telling Jim and Lynn that their work is ineffective. They also miss the opportunity to learn whether there are valid reasons Jim and Lynn behave as they do. Over time, the team's working relationships, and probably its performance, are likely to deteriorate further. This doesn't strike me as particularly effective or compassionate.

You might be thinking, "Why do I have to raise it with the team? Why can't I just talk with Lynn or Jim alone?" Because when you raise the issue one-on-one with Lynn, you assume that your view about Lynn's behavior is accurate and that all the team members agree with you. If Lynn thinks that others might see it differently, you are unilaterally imposing a solution by not taking the issue to the team. Also, Lynn may well believe that her behavior results, in part, from other team members not following through on their tasks.

In addition, if you and Lynn arrive at a solution, and Lynn changes her behavior, other members will wonder what has happened. Now you have created another undiscussable issue—the solution—on top of the original one.

Although undiscussable issues that involve the team ultimately need to be addressed with the team, you can start outside the team. You might approach Lynn and Jim, saying that you have concerns about how their work is affecting you and the team in general. You can also state that you didn't want to raise this issue initially with the team because you didn't want them to feel defensive. Instead, you want to jointly develop with them a way to raise the issue with the team that meets their needs and yours.

Although discussing undiscussable issues is emotionally more difficult than the other behaviors, mechanically speaking, there is nothing new to how it is done. To discuss undiscussable issues, you use all the rest of the behaviors. You state your views and ask genuine questions, share relevant information and give specific examples, test assumptions and inferences, jointly design next steps, and so on. Perhaps the most important element of discussing undiscussable issues is to approach them with compassion and avoid making premature negative judgments about how others acted or why they acted that way.

Again, by undiscussable issues I mean issues that are relevant to your team's work and have a negative impact on your team, but that team members don't address in the team. Here are some undiscussable issues that my clients have faced:

- A CEO has replaced almost every one of his direct reports—some of them more than twice; yet his direct reports have not talked with him—as a team—about how his leadership has contributed to the high team turnover and the resulting financial challenges for the organization.
- A VP thinks his leadership team isn't behaving accountably on its duty to focus on strategic issues, but the VP tries to get them to see this problem themselves, without his raising the issue directly.
- A team of C-Level leaders haven't told the head of organization development that the organization is bringing in outside consul-

tants because leaders don't think OD has the ability to work at senior levels.

Undiscussable issues arise and persist when team members don't use the mutual learning core values. Members aren't transparent or openly curious about issues that significantly affect them. They don't hold each other accountable about these issues, which prevents the team from making an informed choice about how to deal with the issues.

The Cost of Undiscussable Issues

If two team members, Greg and Lori, are concerned that two other members, Erica and Peter, are keeping the team from meeting its fiscal year goals, the issue gets discussed in a number of places. On the way to team meetings, Greg and Lori will likely complain to each other about Erica and Peter. During the meeting, they'll exchange knowing glances as Erica and Peter act in ways that delay the team from making key decisions. Neither Greg nor Lori will say anything in the meeting, but as soon as the meeting is over, they may join up again to privately continue complaining to each other. They may share their concerns with their manager and others so that their concerns about Erica and Peter have become an open secret, known to everyone but Erica and Peter. Assuming that the team is interdependent with Erica and Peter, no resolution can occur until the issue gets addressed with the entire team.

Discussing Undiscussable Issues in Your Team

You've already learned most of what you need to know to discuss undiscussable issues. The skill set and mindset you need for raising undiscussable issues are the same as those you use for any other conversation. What makes discussing undiscussable issues more challenging is the emotions you feel—frustration, anger, disappointment, shame, or fear, to name but a few. This often leads team members to avoid taking accountability for raising and discussing undiscussable issues.

As I said in Chapter Three, in mutual learning teams, members take accountability for raising undiscussable issues. They don't ignore them and they don't try to shift the job to the leader of the team. When they raise an undiscussable issue that they think may have an impact on the entire team, ultimately they discuss the issue in the entire team.

Remaining curious and compassionate makes a big difference when discussing undiscussable issues. Whether you are the team's formal leader or just a member, here are six key steps you can follow:

Step 1: State the issue you want to talk about and your reasoning for discussing it.

Step 2: If relevant, share your concerns about risk and try to reduce it.

Step 3: If appropriate, ask if the others are willing to discuss it.

Step 4: Jointly design how you will have the conversation.

Step 5: Bring the conversation to the team if you didn't raise it there initially.

Step 6: Repeat steps 1–4 with the team.

Step 1: *State the issue you want to talk about and your reasoning for discussing it.* The best way to begin talking about an undiscussable issue is to immediately name the issue. Start the meeting with a clear statement about the undiscussable issue—don't bury the lead. If you ease into the topic, your anxiety and the anxiety of everyone else continues to build as they try to figure out what your concerns are. Naming the issue immediately gets others and you over this emotional hump of uncertainty and anxiety.

If you're the team leader and you're concerned that your direct reports aren't sharing accountability for team decisions, say so. The general formula is as simple as, "I'd like to talk with you about X because Y." In practice, you might say something like, "I'm concerned that I'm taking more accountability for this team than you as a group and that it's not healthy for us in the long term. I want us to talk about this because I'm concerned it's slowing the team's ability to respond quickly to opportunities in the market."

In a team that is experienced in mutual learning, it's not necessary to talk to individual team members before raising the undiscussable issue in the entire team. But for many teams, members can easily become defensive if they are the subject of the undiscussable issue and learn about it for the first time when it is raised in a team meeting. Although undiscussable issues that involve the team ultimately need to be addressed with the team, you can start outside the group. If you are Greg and Lori, you might begin by saying, "Erica and Peter, we want to talk with you because we're concerned that you're doing some things that are making it difficult for us to make sure we hit the team's fiscal year goals. We think that other team members might be feeling the same way, but we didn't want to raise the issue initially with the team because we didn't want to make you defensive. Instead, we'd like to talk with you about what we're seeing and then jointly develop a way for the four of us to raise the issue with the full team so that it works for all of us. We realize we only have part of the story and we're open to the possibility that we may be contributing to the very problem we're concerned about."

Step 2: *If relevant, share your concerns about risk and try to reduce it.* Issues often become undiscussable because people are concerned about possible repercussions. If you lead the team, you may be concerned that raising undiscussable issues with your team will lead the team members to withdraw and make the situation worse. If you're a team member harboring an undiscussable issue about your leader, you may be concerned about the loss of your credibility or reputation, lack of career or financial advancement, possible damage to your relationship with your boss, or loss of employment through downsizing or other methods.[5] If you are a team member with an issue about other team members, you may be concerned that you will lose the support of the team members you have to work with.

The challenge is that your concerns are often based on untested inferences, assumptions, and attributions about what the person has done or will do if you raise the issue you want to raise. If you want to raise an issue about your boss, you may have heard that others who raised similar issues found themselves with a more difficult relationship with the boss or felt marginalized in some way.

Your concern about raising the issue is an undiscussable issue within the undiscussable issue. When you name your concerns, you make it possible to address them and to make a more informed choice about how to proceed.

To raise your concern you might begin by saying something like, "Before I talk with you about this issue, I'm concerned I might be taking a risk by raising it with you. I'd like to describe the risk I think I may be taking and see what assurance, if any, you can offer me."

At some point you'll need to make a judgment call about whether it is worth taking the risk of discussing the undiscussable issue. When considering this, leaders mistakenly emphasize the downside of raising the issue and minimize the potential upside of discussing the issue.

Step 3: *If appropriate, ask if the others are willing to discuss it.* If you don't already have an agreement to discuss undiscussable issues, then ask, "Are you willing to talk about this?" If you are talking to your direct reports, a more appropriate question is, "Is this a good time to talk about this?" Part of the obligation of reporting to someone is to address issues that they bring to you.

Step 4: *Jointly design how you will have the conversation.* As with any conversation, after you have agreed on the purpose, jointly design how you will have the conversation. If you are Greg and Lori you might say, "We'd like for us to agree on how we can have this conversation so it works for all of us. What we'd like to do is start off by giving you some specific examples of our concerns, and then talk about the impact that we think it's having. If you remember the examples differently or if you see the impact differently, let's talk about it and see if we can come to an agreement. Ultimately, we'd like to come to an agreement about how we will bring this to the team. We're open to the possibility that we may be missing things and that we and others may be contributing to the problem. How does that sound as a way to move through the meeting?"

Step 5: *Bring the conversation to the team if you didn't raise it there initially.* Assuming that you didn't initially raise the issue in the full team, the next step is to bring the issue to the team based on the joint design you reached in your meeting. In the current example, Lori, Greg, Erica, and Peter together would bring the issue to the full team.

Step 6: *Repeat steps 1–4 with the team.* The four team members would raise the issue that they want to talk with the team about and summarize the meeting that the four of them already had. This ensures that everyone on the team has the same relevant information. At this point, Lori, Greg, Erica, and Peter would repeat steps 1–4 with the entire team.

I used to say that who is sleeping with whom is not an undiscussable issue—it's gossip—because an undiscussable issue has to be directly related to the team's effectiveness. That was until I was consulting with the VP of sales for a high-tech company. The VP, whom I'll call Roz, was working with her team to prepare for the annual conference that was the single largest sales generator for her organization. The team needed to work closely together to manage the conference work. Unfortunately, two members of the team were not talking with each other because one member had been having an affair with the other member's wife. Most if not all of the team members knew about the situation. The team members tried to act as if nothing was happening, but communication and planning were breaking down. Roz feared that the team would get to the conference, not make sales, and miss the company's revenue targets.

As much as Roz didn't want to raise the issue, she realized that not raising the issue was a bigger risk. First she spoke with the two team members who were directly involved in the affair. She told them why the team needed to deal with this issue. Then together they met with the full team. The focus of the conversation was to jointly figure out how they were going to work together closely in this challenging situation. To identify the problem and plan how to address it, the team had to discuss the undiscussable—the affair—but the heart of the conversation was about how to work together.

A SUMMARY OF BEHAVIORS

Here is a quick summary of the four mutual learning behaviors covered in Chapter Five:

5. Focus on interests, not positions.
   - Four steps to building commitment:
     1. Identify interests.
     2. Agree on interests to consider in the solution.
     3. Craft solutions that meet the interests.
     4. Select a solution and implement it.
   - Listing pros and cons doesn't work.
   - Be careful about saying, "Don't come with a problem unless you have a solution."
6. Test assumptions and inferences.
   - Stay aware of your ladder of inference.
   - Test your own inferences.
   - Test inferences as a team.
7. Jointly design next steps.
   - Put purpose before process before content.
   - Keep the meeting on track.
   - Resolve disagreements over facts.
8. Discuss undiscussable issues.
   - Understand the cost of undiscussable issues.
   - Follow a process for preparing to discuss and then discussing these issues.
     1. State the issue you want to talk about and your reasoning for discussing it.

2. If relevant, share your concerns about risk and try to reduce it.

3. If appropriate, ask if the others are willing to discuss it.

4. Jointly design how you will have the conversation.

5. Bring the conversation to the team if you didn't raise it there initially.

6. Repeat steps 1–4 with the team.

Look back now also at the list at the end of Chapter Four to review the full breadth of behaviors covered here. Remember that the purpose of the eight behaviors is to put the mutual learning mindset into action. The power of the approach stems from the mindset. If you apply the behaviors without it, others will think you've found a new, more sophisticated way to be unilateral—and they'll be right.

6

Designing for Mutual Learning

W ho do you think plays the most influential role in a ship's performance? Most people would name the captain, the engineer, or the navigator. But I'd argue that the most influential role is the ship's architect—the designer. How the architect designs the ship determines how fast and far it can travel, how quickly it can turn, and how well it can protect its crew while withstanding rough seas. The design determines the limits of the ship's performance. Of course, the talent of the crew and the way they work together determine how close they can get to reaching the limits of the design. But no matter how good the captain and crew are, they can't perform better than the ship's design allows. To do that, they have to change some element of the design.

That's exactly what another ship-building industry has done— the airplane industry. If you've been flying since before 1998, you've probably noticed that older planes are being retrofitted with winglets: extensions at the end of each wing that turn up (or up and down) almost ninety degrees. It turns out that with this small change in the design of the wing, the plane can fly a greater distance, climb faster with less noise, and use less fuel.

It's similar with your team. How you design—or redesign—your team determines the limits of its performance. But unlike ships and airplanes, teams don't have physical components to redesign. Instead, teams have *structures* and *processes*—ways members interact with each other in similar patterns over and over. When you establish the roles that your team members will play and the basis on which they'll be rewarded, you're designing structures. When you and your team reach agreement on how the team will solve problems, make decisions, and manage conflicts, you're designing processes. Some structures and processes are formal: your team has explicitly agreed on them. Others are informal; they have developed without discussion. In either case, the structures and processes exist only as long as the team keeps repeating the behaviors that embody them. Stop those behaviors and the structures and processes disappear.

Is your team designed to face its challenges? With a solid design, a team can tackle the demands on it, sustain high performance, improve its working relationships, and provide well-being for team members.

These days the demands on leadership teams are greater than ever. If yours is like most leadership teams, you're facing complex situations that require members to bring and integrate a lot of information and different points of view and make decisions quickly. The situations you face are multifaceted; no one has all the answers. Each team member may be very smart, but to excel as a team at high-stakes decisions, you all have to learn from and with each other. The opportunities for conflict are great. The design choices you make determine in large part whether your team can address the challenge.

WATCH YOUR MINDSET AS YOU DESIGN

Team design embeds core values and assumptions in the team's structure and process, and every element of team design reflects the mindset of the person or people designing it. If you use a unilateral control mindset routinely in challenging situations, chances are you've designed at least part of your team using that same mindset. That means that embedded in your team design are one or more of the unilateral control core values and assumptions—even if that wasn't your intent.

The problem with designing your team using a unilateral control mindset is that, as discussed in Chapter Two, unilateral control creates the results you're trying to avoid. It responds to the demands that your team faces by reducing the level of information available to all team members, by discouraging members from being curious, by reducing the team's ability to make informed choices, and by reducing team members' accountability to one another. This in turn leads to lower performance, weaker working relationships, and lower team member well-being.

Performance assessment processes provide a wealth of examples. For instance, one organization I work with emphasizes that the performance discussion with a direct report should be a conversation—the manager should learn what the direct report is thinking. That's an example of espousing mutual learning. But the process is designed so that, before actually meeting with the direct report, the manager assesses that person's performance, generates examples to support the conclusion, and drafts an improvement plan. At no point in the process is there a place to ask the direct report for a possible different view of the assessment or anything the manager may be missing. And even if there were, it's hard to be curious about what direct reports think about their performance after following a process that's assigned them a performance score.

Other organizations make it even harder to be curious. They require that the manager's leader sign off on assessments of a direct report's performance before the conversation with the direct report. This preemptive oversight is supposed to ensure that leaders assign fair performance ratings. But it also makes it much harder to be curious about what direct reports think, because if it were to turn out that the assessment had missed some significant elements of the direct report's performance, the manager would need to go back to the leader with the correction and say that person deserved a higher rating after all. With a process designed like this, managers' curiosity easily gives way to defending their initial assessment.

In other teams, the assumption guiding the performance assessment design is that the leader doing the evaluation is not contributing to the problem. As a result, if a direct report starts to talk about how things would have gone better had the leader done some things differently, the process essentially demands that the leader steer the conversation away from that issue and back to the direct report's performance. In doing so, the process fails to recognize that the direct report's performance is influenced by the working relationship between the two. So it fails to recognize the leader's accountability for part of the relationship.

In many teams the leader's assessment of a direct report comes from information that is provided by the direct report's peers. But there's no place in the process where the leader shares that or reveals the source of the information. As a result, team members aren't accountable to one another.

Just as you're usually unaware of how you're using your mindset to design behavior, you're unaware of how you're using your mindset to design elements of the team.

Just as you're usually unaware of how you're using your mindset to design behavior, you're unaware of how you're using your mindset to design elements of the team. You don't set out to design your team in a way that may undermine its effectiveness; it's just how your mental operating system works. That's one reason leaders are often surprised when their teams aren't consistently following the core values they espouse. The team's design reflects a different set of values and assumptions than the ones its leader and members fondly believe they're espousing.

In addition to structures and processes, team design involves shaping the general context in which the team exists. Figure 6.1 reiterates the connection between mindset and team design, and the results that they create, and previews the discussion in the rest of this chapter.

THE BIG PICTURE: STRUCTURE, PROCESS, AND CONTEXT

Team structure includes the relatively stable characteristics of a team. When people think of structure, they usually think first of organizational structure—who reports to whom. But a team's structure also includes its mission and vision, its membership, and the roles that each person plays.

Team process is how things are done rather than what is done. To be effective, teams need to manage a number of processes, including how they solve problems and make decisions. And it turns out that much of what constitutes structure is simply a stable, recurring process that emerges from team members continually interacting with each other in the same way.[1]

Team context includes larger organizational elements that influence how the team works. This includes how clear the organization's mission is, how supportive the organization's culture is, and the extent to which the organization's reward system is consistent with the team's objectives and the way it works together.

Remember, a team is a system. To get the best team results, all the elements that constitute it need to be congruent with each other and with the team's mindset.

As the formal leader, you have more authority to design certain team elements than others. Usually leaders have the authority to design their own team process—for example, how the team makes decisions, solves problems, and handles conflicts. That's because team processes usually focus on the internal workings of the team. When

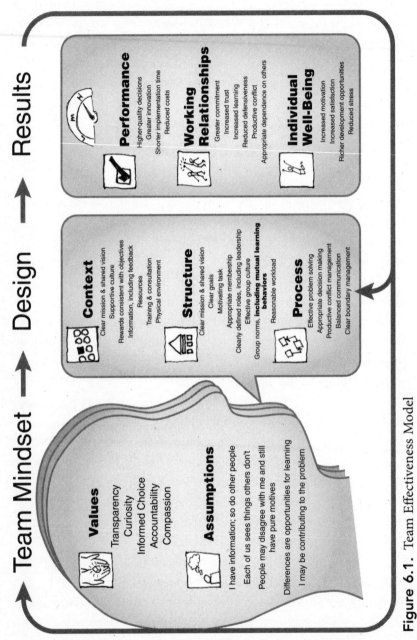

Team Mindset → Design → Results

Team Mindset

Values
Transparency
Curiosity
Informed Choice
Accountability
Compassion

Assumptions
I have information; so do other people
Each of us sees things others don't
People may disagree with me and still have pure motives
Differences are opportunities for learning
I may be contributing to the problem

Design

Context
Clear mission & shared vision
Supportive culture
Rewards consistent with objectives
Information, including feedback
Resources
Training & consultation
Physical environment

Structure
Clear mission & shared vision
Clear goals
Motivating task
Appropriate membership
Clearly defined roles, including leadership
Effective group culture
Group norms, **including mutual learning behaviors**
Reasonable workload

Process
Effective problem solving
Appropriate decision making
Productive conflict management
Balanced communication
Clear boundary management

Results

Performance
Higher-quality decisions
Greater innovation
Shorter implementation time
Reduced costs

Working Relationships
Greater commitment
Increased trust
Increased learning
Reduced defensiveness
Productive conflict
Appropriate dependence on others

Individual Well-Being
Increased motivation
Increased satisfaction
Richer development opportunities
Reduced stress

Figure 6.1. Team Effectiveness Model

Source: Roger Schwarz & Associates; used with permission.

it comes to team structure, you probably have the authority to set team goals and roles, but you may need to establish the team's mission in collaboration with your boss—and perhaps with others, if your organization uses a matrix structure. Finally, the extent to which you influence the team's context depends on your ability to garner resources and influence dynamics in the larger organization. The more senior your leadership team, the more ability you have to do this.

Each of these elements—structure, process, and context—contributes to a team's results, and the mutual learning mindset makes a difference to each of them. But before turning to these details, important as they are, it's useful to consider the most basic team structure question: Is your team in fact a team?

IS YOUR TEAM A REAL TEAM?

You don't always need a leadership team to accomplish the work. What matters is that how the group is structured is congruent with the degree of interdependence among its members. If people aren't really interdependent with each other, then a real team isn't necessary and the leader can simply make decisions after meeting individually with members or even in the group. But if the team members really are interdependent, then not functioning as a real team will reduce its effectiveness.

For example, I once worked with Ted Burton (I have changed the client's name

If people aren't really interdependent with each other, then a real team isn't necessary and the leader can simply make decisions after meeting individually with members or even in the group. But if the team members really are interdependent, then not functioning as a real team will reduce its effectiveness.

at his request), a global transportation company VP who, with his team of twenty-two members, was responsible for the organization's fleet maintenance and repair. His organization was facing several challenges, including supply chain problems that were costing about $250 million a year. He was convinced that this was not a technical problem; instead he believed it was a by-product of the way his team was (or wasn't) working together.

I met with Ted and his team and we discussed the problems they faced and how I might be able to help them. During our conversation it became clear to me that the team faced a more fundamental problem. Finally, I said to the group, "I think the most basic problem you face is that you're not a real team." I then explained that the team members didn't have a basic task around which they considered themselves interdependent. After the meeting, Ted told me he was really annoyed when I said that in the meeting, but he realized that my comment was true. His team wasn't a real team.

A number of months later, Ted told me that he had finally accepted that he didn't have a real team. He also realized—and another type of consulting firm verified it—that many of his direct reports were not interdependent. They were running what were essentially separate businesses and had little need for integrating their work. As a result, Ted rethought his need to have a team that included everyone he'd originally brought in. Once he slimmed down the group to the people who did need to depend on one another, he had a team that could work as a team.

Three criteria for knowing whether a team is real:

- Members are interdependent around a real team task.
- Membership is clearly defined.
- Membership is stable.[2]

The Team Has a Team Task

In a real team, team members work together to identify and solve problems, give advice, and make collaborative decisions. Members are interdependent with each other around the team's task—and they see themselves that way. They understand that the issues they address have an impact on each member's area as well as on the larger organization. As a result, while they take into account the interests of their own areas, they make decisions that meet the larger organization's interests. As one VP said to his team, "I expect that each of you will sacrifice your own budget if it means that we can advance the overall division." To be a real team there has to be real team work to do.

Many so-called leadership teams don't have real team work to accomplish. For example, a leadership team whose members run different businesses with little overlap in markets, products, customers, and technology may have little interdependence, especially if the organization is not undergoing a change in strategy. Similarly, a group of sales directors, each with responsibility for meeting a portion of the Sales VP's goal, may have little interdependence. If each sales director can meet individual goals without affecting others' goals, they're not interdependent. To be interdependent the VP and directors would need to be collectively responsible and collectively accountable for whether and how all the sales goals are met—their own individual goals as well as those of others.

Other leadership teams have a different problem. The members are interdependent, but don't see it.

Members Know Who's on the Team

If team members are going to be interdependent, then they need to know who is on the team and who is not. One study by Richard Hackman and his colleagues found that fewer than 7 percent of the leadership teams they studied, when asked, could agree on who was on the team.[3] And it's not just a problem for team members; I have worked with senior executives who could not tell me exactly who was on the leadership team they led!

In my experience, when the team membership is unclear, the team actually has two subgroups: a core group that certainly belong and everyone agrees that this is so, and a group of associates who may or may not be members, but they themselves aren't sure, other members aren't sure, or both. Team membership can be unclear for a number of reasons. For example, the leader has never formally designated the team; or has shifted people to new roles but is reluctant to move them off or onto the leadership team; or has kept a member off the team who, organizationally, would be expected on it. Whatever the cause, the lack of clarity undermines the team.

The Team Membership Is Stable

Finally, a real team needs to have a stable membership (of course it also helps if the individual members are stable). It takes time for a team to understand and agree on its purpose, agree on how it will work together, and then put those agreements into action, improving them over time. If members are regularly joining and leaving the team, the team doesn't get to benefit from the foundation members created with each other; members spend too much time orienting newcomers and learning how to work together.

Real Team or Team in Name

You can tell when a team is a team in name only. Members don't see the need to attend team meetings because they consider them a waste of their time. When they do attend, they often tune out, not participating unless the topic focuses on their particular part of the business. When members do participate, they represent their own interests rather than focus on the needs of the overall business. At other times, they are quiet or engaged on their smartphones. Members display little curiosity and accountability because they don't see that anything substantial is in play. One leadership team member I work with captured this distinction when he asked his team, "Are we a gymnastics team or are we a hockey team?"

Before your team can work on increasing its effectiveness, it needs to make sure it's a real team. Ask yourself, "Does my team meet the criteria for being a real team?" If your team is a real team, then you can look at how your team's structure makes a difference. (And if it isn't, you can improve everyone's well-being by either making it into a real team or agreeing that you're a group and letting the members attend to their own business.)

TEAM STRUCTURE

These are the elements of an effective team structure:

- Clear mission and shared vision
- Clear goals
- Motivating task
- Appropriate membership
- Clearly defined roles, including leadership
- Effective group culture
- Group norms, including mutual learning behaviors
- Reasonable workload

Clear Mission and Shared Vision

The mission is the purpose of your team; it answers the question "Why do we exist?" Your team achieves its mission by accomplishing various goals, which in turn are achieved by performing various tasks. A vision is a mental picture of the future that an organization seeks to create. Whereas a mission clarifies why the team exists, a vision identifies what your team should look like and how it should act as it seeks to accomplish its mission. Together, a mission and a vision provide meaning that can inspire and guide members' work. I've seen many teams with mission and vision statements on their conference room walls. But the value of mission and vision lies in the shared commitment that members make to achieving them, not in the laminated poster on a wall.

Ultimately, it's your responsibility as the team leader to confirm the mission for the team. But as a mutual learning leader, you don't simply lay out a compelling mission and then expect people to sign up for the trip. Using the mutual learning mindset, you're transparent not only about what the mission is but why it's that mission as opposed to other plausible missions. You're also curious about others' views of the mission, and you seek to incorporate their interests and ideas. When others make suggestions that you finally decide not to incorporate into the mission, you are accountable for explaining your reasoning. You also ask team members to be accountable by saying whether they are willing to commit to the final version of the mission you and the team developed. The idea that members are committed to the team's mission simply because they are on the team is too big an assumption to leave untested.

Ultimately, mission and vision are personal. For team members to commit to them, the mission and vision need to speak to them directly. When members aren't able to commit to the mission and what's required of them to achieve it, you respond with compassion rather than seeing this as an act of insubordination or organizational treason. At the same time, you help those members find another team where they can commit to the mission.

Clear Goals

The team's goals need to be clear enough that members agree on what they mean and can measure progress toward them. The team's goals also need to be consistent with the larger mission and vision. In a mutual learning team, the goals are set with (if not by) the whole team so that members are making an informed choice—a choice they will commit to and accept accountability for. Studies show that when asked to select their own goals, leaders with high needs for achievement typically set challenging goals—ones they have about a 50 percent chance of achieving.[4]

Motivating Task

Even when they are interdependent with each other, team members can become disengaged because the team task isn't motivating. One senior leader who became part of a newly formed corporate-wide project team remarked to me that the project team leader was wasting the team's talent by simply telling the team what to do and how to do it. The team leader was passionate about the project, but he was designing the team's task in a way that demotivated the team. What makes a team task motivating isn't how charismatic or compelling you are as a leader; it's the design of the team task itself. Some teams design members' work in ways that doing it becomes uninteresting; other teams design their work so that doing the work is itself motivating. For a team task to be motivating, it should meet the following conditions:[5]

- It requires members to use a variety of skills.
- It involves a whole and meaningful piece of work with a visible outcome.
- Its outcomes have significant consequences, either for customers or for others in the organization.
- It gives members significant autonomy over how they accomplish the task so that they feel ownership of their work.
- It generates regular and trustworthy feedback to team members about how well the team is performing.

For the team leader, providing informed choice means enabling the team to jointly design the task. It's difficult to know the variety of skills that members have and want to use, what they consider a meaningful piece of work, and what they consider autonomy. By jointly designing the task with the team and being curious, you increase the chance that the task meets these conditions.

Appropriate Membership

An effective team has a carefully selected membership. Members bring a mix of knowledge and skills that will allow them to complete the team's goals successfully. The team should also be just large enough to handle the task. Every added member requires the team to spend additional time coordinating activities. A team with more members than it needs to complete the task will spend time on coordination that could be spent working directly on the task. In addition, as the team grows, members can lose interest in the work and reduce their effort.[6] Some leadership teams contain so many business unit and functional leaders that they're unable to coordinate their work, let alone create the time for members to fully explore different views.

In a team with a unilateral control mindset, the topic of team membership is out of bounds. It's a matter for the team leader alone to consider. But in a team with a mutual learning mindset, members openly discuss whether they have the right mix of people on the team to accomplish their goals.

As discussed earlier in this chapter, a real team must also have clear understanding of who is on the team and a team membership that is stable enough to have the time to learn how to work together well.

Clearly Defined Roles, Including Leadership

In many leadership teams, team members consider the formal leader—the official head of the team—responsible for the team and the formal leader takes on this role. As a result, the formal leader leads the meetings, sets team agendas, guides the flow of discussion, and identifies next steps. Members participate, but leave the leadership roles to the formal leader. If you've led a team like this, even if the team accomplished its goals, you probably had a nagging feeling that you were working harder in the meetings than others—and you were right.

In teams using mutual learning, team member roles are more fluid. Members may rotate chairing the meetings, taking responsibility for coordinating agendas, and identifying next steps. More important, leadership isn't confined to the formal leader. It's a shared role and responsibility. Operating from the assumption that each person may see things that others miss, each member is accountable for ensuring that the team is functioning well. When you see something happening in the team that may reduce its effectiveness, it's your role to raise it with the team, whether you are a team member or the team leader.

Effective Team Culture

Culture is powerful but intangible. It's the set of values and assumptions that team members share and that guide their behavior. Your team's culture can influence how it deals with quality, timeliness, authority, or any other issue relevant to the team's work. For example, one leadership team I worked with held the belief that if you give intelligent people the right information and let them do their work, they will produce a great product. Unsurprisingly, they had very few complaints of micromanaging. People were given a large amount of autonomy, and they produced innovative solutions that met their customer's needs. In contrast, other organizations have a belief that people need to be told exactly what to do, otherwise negative consequences can result. In these organizations, team members have little autonomy and feel underutilized.

The core values and assumptions that constitute your team's mindset can also be considered part of your team's culture, but I have identified them separately because they are so fundamental that they influence how your team engages other aspects of its culture. Still, it's fair to say that changing a team's mindset is changing a team's culture.

You can't identify your team's culture simply by listening to what members (or you) say they value or believe. People can espouse values and beliefs inconsistent with their actions—and be quite unaware of the inconsistencies.[7] The values and beliefs that constitute the team's culture have to be inferred by observing the artifacts of the culture, including how members act.[8] *Artifacts* are products of the culture, including the policies, procedures, and structures that members create.

Culture affects most everything a team does and gets reinforced through policies and behavior, but it generally operates outside team members' awareness, which makes it difficult to identify and change. Mutual learning teams understand the power of culture.

They understand that how the team thinks is how it leads. So they talk about the culture that they want to create and how it may differ from their current team culture. They identify the values and assumptions that are currently operating in the team and openly discuss whether they are helping or hindering the team. They are always asking themselves, "How does the decision or action we're about to take align with the values and assumptions we say we stand for?" This often involves discussing undiscussable issues, as described in Chapter Five. Once team members have identified gaps between their present culture and their desired culture, they jointly design ways to close this gap.

Group Norms, Including Mutual Learning Behaviors

Norms are expectations that team members share about how they should behave with each other. Norms come from the team's culture. They are ways of putting the culture into action. One easily observed norm involves time. (Throughout the world, time is treated differently in different cultures.) For example, some leadership teams I work with place a high value on the precision of time and assume that honoring time commitments conveys respect. As a result they have a norm that meetings start exactly at the designated starting time, regardless of who is absent. Other teams I work with have different values and assumptions about time. They have developed a norm that leads them to start meetings after everyone arrives, which could be fifteen minutes later than planned.

Unfortunately, team norms often develop implicitly, just like the values and assumptions that give rise to them. When that happens, your team finds itself operating with a set of expectations that mysteriously evolved over time and may not serve its needs.

The behaviors described in Chapters Four and Five are, in effect, norms that put the mutual learning core values and assumptions into action. When your team adopts them, they become norms for how team members will work together. Just as smart teams discuss and agree on the core values and assumptions they want to guide their team, they also explicitly discuss what expectations they have for each other. Because they are transparent about the norms and make an informed choice about adoption, they are able to hold each other accountable when they see others acting in ways that don't meet a team expectation. In fact, in mutual learning teams, it's a norm that all team members give feedback when they think others are acting inconsistently with a team expectation. In this way, team members share accountability for supporting each other in creating the behaviors they have agreed will lead to better results.

The mutual learning behaviors are a set of norms that describe critical behaviors for team effectiveness, but teams can have norms about anything, including how to dress, how to manage time, and how to use team space. Smart teams explicitly discuss these norms as well, ensuring that they are putting expectations in place that will serve them well.

Reasonable Workload

Although teams can achieve incredible results and consistently exceed expectations, they still have limits to what they can accomplish in a finite amount of time. And while technology has increased performance speed for many functions, it hasn't increased the speed at which human beings think or work with others—two central tasks for leaders and leadership teams. Effective teams have the ability to estimate when the demands on their time will become so great that the quality of their work will begin to suffer. More important, teams that are able to raise undiscussable issues explicitly address this when they see it coming.

TEAM PROCESS

Team process refers to how things are done rather than what is done.[9] To be effective, teams must manage a number of processes. The two primary team processes are problem solving and decision making, but conflict management, communication, and establishing boundaries are also important.

Effective Problem Solving

Leadership teams spend much of their time solving problems. A problem is simply a gap between what is desired and what exists. Problem solving is the systematic approach a team uses to work through a logical set of steps.

Teams have access to many systematic processes for solving problems, such as Lean, Six Sigma, and other process improvement methods. All of these methods can be very powerful, but only if team members are willing to be transparent, curious, accountable, and compassionate with each other. If team members withhold information or assume that they are right and others are wrong, these problem-solving processes become unilateral control battlegrounds. Teams that use some formal type of problem-solving process are typically more skilled at the technical side than at raising challenging issues. As a result, they end up trying to solve problems without all the relevant information.

Appropriate Decision Making

When people first learn about mutual learning, they often assume that they'll need to make decisions by consensus. It isn't so. The difference between being a mutual learning leader and a unilateral control leader isn't the kind of decision-making rules you use—it's your mindset.

As a simple exercise, consider three basic approaches to decision making: consensus, team input, and individual. In consensus everyone agrees to support a particular solution. In team input, the leader gets input from the group (or individuals within the group) before making the decision. In the individual approach, the leader makes the decision

> *The difference between being a mutual learning leader and a unilateral control leader isn't the kind of decision-making rules you use—it's your mindset.*

without getting input from team members. Both unilateral control leaders and mutual learning leaders can apply each approach and come up with differing outcomes.

If you use unilateral control to approach a consensus decision, you act as if you're thinking, *How do I get my team members to buy in to the solution that I have already developed?* If you're using mutual learning you act as if you're thinking, *How do I ensure that we get a decision that is based on valid information that ideally meets all stakeholders' needs?* The solution may be one that you thought of before the meeting, one that another team member suggested, or one that the team jointly crafts in the meeting.

With the team input approach, if your mode is unilateral control, you assume that you understand the situation and are right. When team members offer views or solutions that disagree with yours, you privately question the team members' motives and discount their views. But if you're operating from mutual learning, you assume that team members may see things that you don't, and you openly question team members and try to learn from their various views.

What about the individual approach? Regardless of your mindset, many times you do need to make decisions without consulting others. In these situations, if you're operating from unilateral control, you consider your own needs first and assume you have most or all of the information you need to make a sound decision. You may or may not tell your direct reports about these decisions, let alone how you arrived at them. But if you're using mutual learning, you act as a steward, thinking about all stakeholders' interests. You make these decisions recognizing that you have less than full information. You have a sense of accountability to your direct reports. As a result, you tell your direct reports the decisions you made and the reasoning underlying them. You ask if your decision may create any problems, recognizing that, in some situations, you may not be able to change the decision.

If you've already made a decision, you tell people so. You don't go through the charade of getting input if you've made up your mind.

Many leaders have learned that it's important to get input and engage people in decisions because it leads to greater commitment. So even when they've made a decision, they go through the motions of getting input—and then implement the decision they had already made. Then they're surprised when team members aren't committed to the decision. These leaders confuse the behavior with the underlying values. They miss the point that seeking input is valuable when it reflects genuine curiosity and openness to change. Seeking input without genuine curiosity and openness to change is manipulative and reduces trust and commitment.

Team members don't expect to be involved in every decision, nor do they want to be. But they do expect you to be transparent with them about whether you've made up your mind about something or how open you are to being influenced. And they expect that you won't waste their time and yours by getting their input on issues you've already decided.

Productive Conflict Management

Smart teams appreciate that conflict is a natural part of team-work and organizations. They understand that conflict is simply what occurs when people advocate for different solutions that can't all be implemented. The mutual learning mindset makes it easier for your team to engage conflict productively. Because members assume that differences are opportunities for learning, they don't dig in to positions and try to win the conflict. Nor do they try to avoid the conflict or simply accommodate others' positions.[10]

Instead, they get curious, engage others, discover the source of their different views, and work to bridge the differences. Bridging the difference is not the same as compromising. When you compromise, you are still operating from a position, seeking to maximize your own gain. When you bridge the difference, you understand where your assumptions differ from others and where your interests are aligned even when your positions are in conflict. This enables the team to generate solutions that aren't possible through compromise. Because team members assume that no one has all the pieces of the puzzle and that people can disagree without having questionable motives, they can address high-stakes conflicts without having them damage working relationships.[11] In fact, mutual learning teams often report that after resolving a high-stakes conflict, they have better a working relationship with the other parties.

Balanced Communication

Teams need to communicate so that members get the information they need and so that the team develops a common understanding of the issues it discusses. Without common understanding, team members can go off in different directions and can create conflicts even when acting with the best of intentions.

The mutual learning approach provides basic principles and specific guidance for balanced and effective communication. By *balanced*, I mean that members communicate directly with the people from whom they need information and with whom they need to solve problems. In many teams, team communication operates from the assumption that members are accountable to the leader. As a result, when challenging situations arise, the leader often serves as the hub of communication, with each member sharing relevant information with the leader. But in mutual learning teams, communication operates from the assumption that each team member is accountable to the full team. As a result, members are accountable for sharing their own information directly with the relevant team members. As the team leader, you don't end up serving as an intermediary for team members who are having conflicts with each other.

Part of the assumptions in many team cultures is that the formal leader, by virtue of having formal authority, gets to play by a different set of rules than the rest of the team members. The leader may control or dominate the meeting, interrupt others, or switch the conversation when it looks like someone is off-track. Other team members may find this behavior ineffective, but they don't raise the issue. But mutual learning teams operate from the assumption that all team members, including the formal leader, play by the same ground rules. That means that behavior that is considered ineffective for a team member is also ineffective for the team leader. This doesn't change the leader's authority to make decisions; it simply requires the use of effective communication behavior in doing so.

Teams that use a mutual learning mindset communicate about a wider range of issues. They discuss issues that other teams are unable or unwilling to discuss. As a result, they address barriers to team effectiveness that are out of reach for members of unilateral control teams. Finally, because they understand that both thoughts and emotions are important for making good decisions, they talk about their feelings as part of problem solving and managing conflict. As a result, team members have a deeper understanding of each other.

Clear Boundary Management

Every team has to figure out how to work with the larger organization it is part of.[12] This means managing the team's boundaries. When your team is working with other teams, it has to figure out where its responsibility for a task ends and other teams' responsibility begins. If your team doesn't manage this boundary well, it can end up taking on tasks that are beyond its expertise, responsibility, or resources; alternatively, your team could end up with other teams performing its work. When your team is working with other teams, it also needs to figure out who gets to make what decisions.

When your team members seek agreement on these issues with other teams, they do so as peers, not with the authority to unilaterally decide these issues. If your team members can't collaboratively reach agreement on these issues, the issues get escalated to you and your counterparts on the other teams to handle, and the accountability for managing these issues shifts unnecessarily from your team to you. Fortunately, smart teams can resolve these kinds of boundary conflicts with other teams even when the other teams don't know mutual learning.

TEAM CONTEXT

Even if you lead the most senior leadership team in your organization, your team's effectiveness is influenced by the larger organization. The context in which your team works best includes

- A clear *organizational* mission and shared vision
- A supportive culture
- Rewards consistent with team objectives
- Information including feedback
- Material resources
- Training and consultation
- A physical environment that supports the work

Depending on your team's level in the organization, you have at least some influence or control over some of these elements that form the context for your team. In any case, mutual learning teams take an active approach to the larger organizational environment that influences their work. This means changing policies when your team has the authority to do so, influencing policy when you lack the authority, and when you have neither authority nor influence, finding creative ways to minimize the negative effects of the organization on your team.

Clear Organizational Mission and a Shared Vision

Your organization has a mission and vision that serves as the umbrella for all of its teams. It should go without saying that your team's mission and vision should be congruent with that of the larger organization. Still, you may find times when others outside your team are acting in ways that seem at odds with the organization's espoused mission and vision. Mutual learning teams are willing to engage others with curiosity and compassion when this occurs.

As your organization undergoes significant changes in its mission, expect that your team will face challenges. A health care provider that began moving to an accountable care organization model, for example, found that the shift in mission and vision led to structural changes that required the clinical leadership team to redefine its roles and reporting relationships with other key leaders in the organization.

A Supportive Organizational Culture

Just as your team has a culture, so does the larger organization. Teams that work in an organization with a supportive culture have a greater chance of being effective because team members share the basic values and assumptions that guide organizational behavior in general. When your team has a culture at odds with the larger organizational culture, even simple work with other teams can be challenging.

Many organizations espouse values and assumptions similar to mutual learning, but few organizations, including those that espouse this kind of culture, act in ways that demonstrate it. In practice, most organizations' cultures resemble unilateral control to a greater or lesser degree. One organization development manager told me that his organization had a great culture on paper, but that leaders and teams didn't know how to live the culture every day. He saw mutual learning as a way to translate the company's compelling but abstract culture into everyday behavior. You may be in a similar situation.

Then again, your organization may gleefully espouse a culture of unilateral control. If so, the challenge isn't simply developing new behaviors to put the mutual learning culture into action; it also means changing the values and assumptions that are embedded in the organization. As difficult as it is to change your team's culture, it's exponentially more difficult to change the larger organization's culture, if only because of its size. If your team is senior enough, you may decide that the mutual learning core values and assumptions reflect the kind of organization culture that you want your organization to embody. If so, modeling the values and assumptions in your team is a good start for others to learn what is possible.

But even if your team isn't in a position to formally influence the culture of your larger organization, when you work with people outside your team you can influence how they think and act. I've worked with many leaders who, after a particularly challenging but effective meeting, were approached by a leader who said something like, "How did you do that? I've been trying for weeks to get an agreement with that group and you did it in a few hours." By modeling successful mutual learning and having people see the results, you are more likely to encourage people to become curious about how to create similar results. These are opportunities to explain what you were doing and the mindset that made it possible.

Rewards Consistent with Objectives

If you want your team to function as a team, then your organization's reward system needs to be consistent with the way your team produces its outcomes—and it needs to stay consistent. Otherwise, you get unintended consequences, like the one encountered by a graphic design team in a financial company. The team had an excellent reputation, serving its internal customers well and winning industry awards for its designs. Members worked closely together on projects, not concerned about who got credit. The team leader was able to reward the team as a whole for their work—until HR changed the reward system so that each team member had to be rated and ranked individually and given a merit bonus based on individual effort. The team found itself paying attention to who was doing what; henceforth work that had flowed naturally among them now was in contention. To their credit, they recognized that the new reward system compromised their behavior, and they approached HR to describe their concerns and see if their interests could be met. Unfortunately, HR maintained that a team-level reward system was out of the question. They had to divide the performance pay among the team and they couldn't divide it equally. Eventually, most of the team members left to start their own firm.

Rewards do need to be congruent with the values that the organization espouses. When I introduced mutual learning to leaders in a global oil company, I first showed them the unilateral control approach. I asked, "Does anyone recognize this model?" One leader said, "Yeah, that's basically what we use here." Another leader added, "Use it? We've been rewarded for it—I've been rewarded for it—for twenty years!" The organization was concerned about the results that its leadership practices were generating, but no one had realized that it had designed the reward system to reinforce the unilateral control results.

Often organizations hope to create a certain culture even as they reward behaviors that are inconsistent with it.[13] For example, this happens when they design the reward system and other organizational policies that try to reward mutual learning but operate from a unilateral control mindset. Employees are exhorted to be transparent and accountable at the same time Human Resources policy bars discussion of salaries. Leaders receive survey results evaluating their leadership in which the evaluations are anonymous so the leader can't know who has said what and those who said it don't have to be accountable for the accuracy of their statements. Ultimately this leads to cynicism as people see the gap between what the organization says is important and what it rewards and prohibits. And cynicism is a first step toward apathy.

Smart teams identify how organizational systems are rewarding ineffective team behavior and they try to change these systems. Even if your team is unable to change or influence the system, it can discuss the negative consequences and explore ways to minimize the effects.

Information, Including Feedback

Every team needs information from the larger organization to accomplish its objectives and improve the way it works. Information is the lifeblood of informed choice.

Systems Information

As organizations use enterprise resource planning systems, leadership teams increasingly have real-time information about finance

and accounting, manufacturing, sales and service, customer relations, and human resources. These integrated systems can enable
your team to work effectively with others within the organization and
with customers and vendors. Of course, your team's ability to use the
information depends on the quality of the information, the extent to
which it captures data that your team needs, and your ability to access
it. Here too, the organization shows how transparent and accountable
it is by how it enables teams to access this information and by the
extent to which it designs the system to produce the information that
leadership teams need.

Information from Other Teams

But much of the information your team needs isn't embedded in
information systems; it's in the minds of the other teams you work
with. Whether your team is working with another function, with
suppliers, or with customers, your success depends on your ability to
get all the information on the table to make good decisions. Many
leaders I have worked with complain that other teams aren't forth-
coming with information they need. They infer that others are
withholding information. But this often changes when your team
becomes more transparent with its information, more curious about
what the other teams' interests are, and more compassionate
about the other teams' situation. When others understand that you
intend to use their information for them rather than on them, they
become more willing to share what you need.

Feedback from Colleagues

One of the most pervasive ways that larger organizations fail their
teams is by withholding feedback from team members or creating
feedback mechanisms that aren't transparent or accountable. I once
was part of a group of management professors at a university who
often taught in executive development programs. Other (nonmanagement) professors in the school ran these programs. Occasionally
these nonmanagement professors would approach someone else in

the management group to express their concerns about our teaching—but they wouldn't approach the person who had taught for them. To address this problem, my management faculty colleagues and I agreed that we would not allow colleagues to give feedback indirectly—we wanted more accountability.

For example, if I had taught a session that participants had some concerns about, the professor who ran that program—let's call him Larry—would approach my colleague Dick and tell him that he was concerned about my performance. After Dick tested his assumption that Larry hadn't given me this feedback, Dick asked what led him not to talk directly with me. Larry almost always said that he didn't want to upset me—and he'd sometimes add that he wanted Dick to relay the concerns to me without indicating the source.

At this point Dick would ask, "What's your purpose in telling me if you don't want Roger to know?" As we had agreed in our management group, Dick would tell Larry that for the information to be valid enough for me to change, Dick would have to give me specific details, which would make it obvious that it was Larry who had shared the concerns with Dick. And without those details, I would be unlikely, if not unable, to change in exactly the way Larry was suggesting. In short, to meet Larry's interest of doing a better job for his clients, he would need to give me the feedback directly. Dick would offer to coach Larry on how Larry could give me feedback and Dick would even agree to be present to help Larry give me the feedback. If Larry still said he didn't want me to know, Dick would say that he couldn't make an agreement that would withhold important information about my performance. Dick would then tell Larry that he (Dick) planned to give me Larry's feedback and that I would probably come visit Larry to find out firsthand what Larry's concerns were about my performance. When Dick gave me the feedback, I went to Larry's office and, with genuine curiosity, asked about his concerns with my performance. By working in this way, my management colleagues and I taught our other colleagues to be accountable to us directly and we were accountable to them.

Survey Feedback

As I've discussed, 360-degree feedback generally leads to failures of transparency and accountability, because most responses are aggregated and therefore anonymous. The same problems arise when a team is getting 360-degree feedback. For example, the team's boss's feedback is identified, but even the team members don't know how their fellow team members evaluated the team in the survey items.

All of this makes it difficult if not impossible for a team to improve how it performs and works together. If you don't know what your team members think about the team, it's difficult to talk about exactly what team members should do differently to improve it. And it's difficult to be curious because asking people specifically how they rated the team on a particular item violates the agreement that individual responses will be anonymous. The anonymity that leads to lack of transparency, curiosity, informed choice, and compassion stems from the assumptions that granting people anonymity will yield the truth and that it will save face both for those giving the feedback and those receiving it. However, no research has indicated that granting anonymity gets the truth; people can still distort their responses because they aren't accountable.[14] And researchers note that 360-degree feedback doesn't necessarily lead to behavior change.

The anonymity that leads to lack of transparency, curiosity, informed choice, and compassion stems from the assumptions that granting people anonymity will yield the truth and that it will save face both for those giving the feedback and those receiving it.

When your team uses mutual learning with 360-degree feedback, you and your team complete the survey and ask direct reports, peers, and your boss to complete the survey also. When the survey results come back to your team, each team member's responses are identified by name. Those outside the team are asked to sign their surveys so team members can follow up if they have questions. This makes the responses transparent and accountable. It facilitates curiosity and asking your team members what led them to respond as they did and what needs to happen for the team to become more effective in that area. This is the level of conversation that's needed for teams to improve. Can it feel uncomfortable? Yes, at first, but the goal is not to be comfortable—it's to be effective, even as you feel uncomfortable.

Only when those giving you feedback identify themselves can you get to the level of behaviors that are specific enough to create change. My colleague Anne Davidson worked with the senior leadership team of a city. The city manager received anonymous 360-degree feedback from his team that he delegated too much. So he started delegating less. Then his team got frustrated that they weren't being included in decisions. After much upset to the team, Anne facilitated a discussion where the team members were willing to tell the city manager face-to-face what they meant by "over-delegate." The real issue was that he was not providing enough background information on his interests when he delegated, not that they wanted him to delegate less, but the survey provided no way to give that specific feedback—it had a scale that asked about the degree of delegation. With that specific information, the city manager changed his behavior and the team became satisfied with the level of delegation.

If you're thinking that people on your team don't trust each other (or you) enough to be this transparent and accountable, then you've probably identified the most significant problem your team faces. Solve that problem and every other team problem becomes much easier to deal with. If you or your team members believe that you must first have trust before you can start moving to mutual learning, then you are confusing cause and effect, and will probably never build or rebuild trust. Trust develops when team members take risks by making themselves vulnerable—for example, by being transparent—and see that others do not use the vulnerability against them.

Taking the initiative to identify yourself can take some effort. Tom, a director of a large metropolitan library system, found that when he was asked to complete 360-degree evaluations of his peers, the survey granted him anonymity, even though he didn't want it. To take accountability, in the space provided to add comments, Tom wrote his evaluation of the peer and began each comment with "Tom thinks . . ."

Resources

Apart from information, your team needs other resources, including technology and material resources. For virtual teams this includes the technology to work together across time and space. While using mutual learning may not increase your team's ability to obtain additional resources, it can increase the chance that you better understand the reasoning of those providing the resources.

Training and Consultation

Teams periodically need training and consultation to develop their skills and get help solving problems. But the training or consultation your team receives may be at odds with the mutual learning culture you're trying to create. Many leadership teams have told me the different unilateral control techniques they have learned at some point in their careers—either from internal or external consultants. They often mention instruction in the sandwich approach to feedback, talking last so they learn what their team members really believe, and asking rhetorical questions so as to make their points without actually saying anything anyone could argue with.

Often the training and consulting in organization and team development as well as HR espouses mutual learning but provides tools and techniques designed for unilateral control. One organization described its performance management process as a conversation with the employee, but at no time did it teach leaders how to be curious about the inferences they made about the employee or the employee's reactions to the leader's plan for the employee. The problem extends to universities as well. In one executive MBA program, each student was assigned to secretly observe another student. At the end of the semester, the secret observers would share their feedback with the student they were observing. When one student objected to the process because it wasn't transparent, accountable, and didn't provide the observed students with timely information to make informed choices, the faculty member explained that she was mirroring a process that occurs all the time in organizations. But modeling ineffective practices doesn't create effective outcomes.

Teams that focus sharply on their team strategy assess every choice they make by asking if it's congruent with the strategy. If it's not, they make a different choice that is. They know that if they make a decision that's at odds with the team strategy, they will dilute or even undermine their efforts. This is the same approach that mutual learning teams use with training and consultation. Each time they look for training or consultation, they assess the product or service and ask whether it's congruent with the core values and assumptions. They know that it will create problems for the team if it subjects itself to training or consultation methods that aren't.

Physical Environment

Winston Churchill said, "We shape our buildings and then our buildings shape us." The physical environment that your team works in has subtle but powerful effects. One consumer products organization designed its new facility based on the desire to increase collaboration. It designed enclosed and open office spaces to meet the different leaders' needs; informal café-like places with tables and comfortable chairs nears located near stairs, so people could easily start or continue a conversation; a very prominent open staircase to encourage people to walk and therefore meet each other more frequently than on an elevator; conference rooms that people could reserve; and other conference rooms that could only be used spontaneously. All of these environmental decisions stemmed from the organization's specific values and assumptions about encouraging collaboration and spontaneous conversation within teams and across teams.

Contrast that example with a professional development organization that moved into a new building and assigned most of the conference rooms to key leaders, so that others could no longer meet spontaneously. Or, worse, an agricultural manufacturer that found out it had redesigned its building to include almost no spaces for people to meet.

How your team's space is configured reflects the values and assumptions of those who design the space. If you have control over your team's space, ensure that it reflects how the team wants to work together. If you don't have control, seek to influence those decisions or make ad hoc changes so the physical environment facilitates rather than hinders your team's ability to work together.

STAY CONGRUENT

All design decisions—structural, social, and physical—should take their cues from and be congruent with the team's mindset. As much as possible, they should also match the organization's core values and assumptions. Of course, it can be easier to set that goal than to pursue it in real life, but the challenges of creating and maintaining a team based on the mutual learning mindset are well worth addressing.

CHAPTER 7

Dealing With Common Team Challenges

Applying mutual learning in your team changes the way you and the team approach common challenges. That applies to preparing for and conducting meetings, jointly planning and conducting feedback, and working as a team when physically apart, including e-mail communications. It also covers issues such as speaking with one voice to support a decision without suppressing personal concerns, and helping the team to influence you as its leader.[1]

PREPARING FOR MEETINGS

I was coaching a leader who talked about how he prepared for challenging meetings. He described it like a chess game. Before the meeting he would privately review the possible steps the other people might take. He would say to himself, *"If they say A, I'll say X. If they say B, I'll say Y."* He said it was hard to plan like that because plotting so many possible moves took a lot of time and was tiring. I agreed and said that unless you're a Bobby Fischer, it's difficult to think more than a couple of moves ahead and even then there's no guarantee your planning will pay off. More important, if you're planning for a meeting like it's a chess game then you're already thinking in terms of winners and losers. You're playing a unilateral control game.

Fortunately, there's an easier and more productive way to prepare for meetings. It involves asking yourself three basic questions to identify what you need to be transparent about:

- *What relevant information do I need to share?* What information do you have that others need to know? It may be information about what your team has accomplished, problems you're encountering, financial information, or anything else.
- *What interests do I have?* If you're trying to make a decision or solve a problem, identify the interests that any solution needs to meet (discussed in Chapter Five under Behavior 5). Complete this sentence as many times as necessary to get clear about your interests: "No matter what solution we come up with, it needs to be one that . . ." When you're done, you will have a list of interests that you can share in the conversation. This will be much more effective than coming into the meeting with your solution (a position) and trying to convince others to buy it.
- *What assumptions and inferences am I making that I need to test?* Going into the meeting, you're probably making some assumptions and inferences about the problem, the solution, or the other people. You might be inferring that other members aren't as concerned about solving the problem quickly because it has taken a month for them to meet with you. You might be inferring that others have the expertise or authority to implement a solution.

Spend some time becoming aware of your assumptions and inferences (Behavior 6 in Chapter Five) so you can test them out in the meeting. Every incorrect assumption or inference you make undercuts your ability to find a solution that works for you and others. And it can create unnecessary conflict. Complete this sentence as many times as necessary to get clear about your assumptions: "I am assuming that . . ." When you're done, you will have a list of assumptions or inferences that you can test out during the conversation to see if they are valid.

If you turn the three questions you ask yourself around, you will have three important areas to be curious about with others:

- What relevant information do others have to share with me?
- What interests do they have that need to be met?
- What assumptions and inferences are they making?

By being transparent about your information and curious about what others know and think, you lay a foundation for solving problems with others. Regarding how you seek relevant information, if you know that your revenue was off by 10 percent in the last quarter, you can be curious about what they think are the causes. If you've had difficulty hiring talent in your organization, what does HR know about the supply and demand of the pool that you're recruiting from? If you know that others think your projections are unrealistic, be curious about what they know that leads them to that conclusion.

If you know others' positions, be curious about their underlying interests. If they're reluctant to go along with your proposal, get curious about what interests of theirs it doesn't meet.

Before the meeting, think about what relevant information and interests others have. But just as you make assumptions and inferences about others, they do the same with you. So before the meeting also be curious about the assumptions and inferences they may be making about the situation or your team, and prepare to ask about them. In the end, you'll have a list of questions you can ask—not to use against others but to understand how they are seeing things differently. Only when you really understand how their thinking differs from yours can you begin to work on bridging the gap and finding a solution that will work for everyone.

DURING MEETINGS

Three mutual learning guidelines can help you with common challenges during meetings: Go broad before you go deep, don't hold back, and deal with nonverbal behavior.

Go Broad Before You Go Deep

How often do you have a meeting in which your team needs to make a decision, yet only a few people are talking? By the end of the meeting, you have no idea what many of your team members think. In addition, you may have spent the majority of the meeting talking in depth with one or two people on their particular issues, while the rest of the team seems to disengage.

Leadership teams can get stuck when they go deep without first going broad. *Going deep* means following up with a team member to learn more detail about that particular person's thinking on a topic. *Going broad* means finding out briefly what every member thinks about a topic before learning in depth about any team member's views.

Say your team has just started discussing whether to temporarily stop shipping a product because of quality problems. You ask the team members what they think; Sheena responds first, saying, "I don't think the problem is serious enough that we should stop shipping product." Going deep is asking Sheena to further explain her thinking, for example by asking, "What leads you to say the problem isn't serious enough?" Going broad is asking others to share their response to your initial question or to Sheena's answer. For example, "What are others' initial thoughts about whether we should stop shipment at this time?"

If you begin the meeting exploring an issue by going deep with one person, you may learn a lot about what that one team member thinks, but other members quickly begin to get frustrated or bored and you may lose their attention. And the deeper you go with that one team member, the further you may get from the original topic.

If you start by going broad, the entire team will quickly understand what all team members' initial views are, and you will have more information to decide where to go deeper. You keep team members engaged, and you dive deep into details only after identifying where a deep dive is a valuable use of time. As you address various aspects of problems or topics, you may find you need to go broad again, then delve back into the details and then return to the broader conversation. This ensures that as your team gets deeper into exploring the causes of a problem and the potential solutions, the entire team is moving together.

Don't Hold Back

Often leaders tell me they deliberately hold back in their meetings. They say that they really want to know what their direct reports are thinking, but if they (the leaders) speak first, other team members stop expressing different views. The leaders reason that if they hold back and ask their team to speak first, they'll hear more ideas.

This strategy sounds reasonable, but talking last is a unilateral control strategy that can easily generate a unilateral control response. If your team members know your habits and are concerned about not contradicting you, they're likely to hold back as they try to figure out why you aren't sharing your views and what your views are. This, in turn, will lead you to think that your team members haven't thought through the issue or are acting overly cautious, which may lead you to think they are ineffective.

The talk-last strategy also bypasses a deeper issue: What is happening in your team that you have to talk last to avoid influencing what others would otherwise say to you? Rather than bypassing this question, consider raising it with your team. You might say something like, "I want to share a pattern in our team that concerns me and get your reactions. I've noticed that after I share my view on a topic, no one disagrees with me. The discussion just seems to stop. Let me give you some examples [then describe a couple of situations where you observed this pattern]. I'm wondering, what's leading this to happen? I'm asking because I want you to be disagreeing with me but I don't see it happening. I'm curious: Am I doing something that contributes to this?"

You may learn that the reason conversation stops after you express your view is that you do things to stop the conversation. You may state your view without being genuinely curious about what others think; ask rhetorical questions that put people down for their view; or interrupt people when they are saying things that you see differently. Any of these behaviors can lead your direct reports to shut down.

The good news is that once you address the cause of what's keeping your team from engaging in full discussion with you, you won't have to worry about whether you speak first, last, or at any other time.

The good news is that once you address the cause of what's keeping your team from engaging in full discussion with you, you won't have to worry about whether you speak first, last, or at any other time. You'll be able to speak whenever you want without unduly affecting the outcome. That's how it should be.

Dealing with Nonverbal Behavior

You're meeting with your team and you notice people rolling their eyes, folding their arms, pushing back their chairs, or sighing. You think something's wrong but you don't know what.

You can test your inference that something's wrong. If Sean has been looking at his watch and then rolling his eyes each time Nicole speaks, you can say something like this: "Sean, I'd like to check something out. I'm noticing you're looking at your watch and then rolling your eyes while Nicole is speaking. Am I off?" If Sean says you've got it right, then you continue, "I'm thinking that you may have some concern about what Nicole is saying or about something else. Yes?"

If he agrees, you continue, "Would you be willing to say what your concern is?"

To review, when you test an inference you do this: you name the behavior you see and who is doing it; you check out whether it means what you think it means (your inference), and you ask the people involved if they are willing to share their thinking.

A couple of factors make it challenging to intervene on nonverbal behavior. First, when team members show nonverbal behavior that may indicate disagreement or disengagement, it's often because they are reacting negatively to something going on in the team. That means you're commenting on some potential conflict in the team, which you may have a difficult time doing. Second, team members aren't as aware of their nonverbal behavior as they are of what they are saying, so asking about it can feel more intrusive.

These factors can lead you to ignore nonverbal behavior. But by doing so, you miss opportunities to address important team dynamics. If team members' nonverbal behavior represents their frustration, anger, or dissatisfaction with the process and you don't learn about it, you're risking the team's ability to accomplish its goals.

When leaders or other team members do address this situation, many deal with it by not referring to the behavior specifically. For example, if Sean starts looking at his watch and rolling his eyes after Nicole has been talking for several minutes, someone might say, "I just want to check in and see how people are doing." Or they might make a slightly more specific—but still general—comment like, "I'm thinking that people are concerned about the time." Or they may identify the behavior but not the person exhibiting the behavior: "I'm noticing that people are looking at their watches and rolling their eyes." All of these statements do have the effect of saving face for Sean. But for a leader to withhold the information to save face for someone else has an unacceptable consequence. It means you're privately discounting your team's ability to handle the direct feedback and communicating to them that they don't have to be accountable. This makes it harder for them to give each other honest and direct feedback in the future, because you've unilaterally decided to deprive them of the opportunity now. This means you're contributing to the team's ineffectiveness by reinforcing their behavior instead of modeling a more productive alternative.

GIVING FEEDBACK

If you and your team members are going to be transparent with each other, enable each other to make informed choices, and hold each other accountable, then you need to give regular feedback, formally and informally. Volumes have been written about how to give feedback effectively, usually the negative kind. Most recommend you give feedback as soon as possible, make it specific, and stay away from making high-level judgments. That's generally good advice as far as it goes, but it doesn't really go far enough to support real action. Here are some key points for improving your feedback by applying a mutual learning mindset and skill set:

- As you approach the conversation, be open to changing your mind.
- Jointly design the conversation.
- Jointly design the order of the feedback.
- Give people the headlines—don't make them guess.
- Ask about your own contribution—before anyone else raises it.
- If someone seems to get defensive—stay curious!
- Hold others accountable—don't allow anonymous feedback.
- If you don't share the negative feedback soon, don't impose penalties based on it.
- Get feedback on how you're giving feedback.

As you approach the conversation, be open to changing your mind. If you think the purpose of feedback is to convince someone to see it your way or to help them see the light, you're bound to make the other person defensive. If, however, you consider it an opportunity to be transparent about what you've seen and curious about what you may be missing, you can learn a lot—and so can the person you're giving feedback to. Being curious is one of the most powerful things you can do to give feedback effectively. This doesn't mean holding back on what you think; it means being just as curious about the other person's view as you are convinced about your own.

Jointly design the conversation. Everyone knows that if you control the process of the conversation, you can usually control the outcome. If you're receiving feedback, that's a scary thought. Start the conversation by agreeing on the purpose of the conversation and how you will hold it. This reduces everyone's anxiety and also lets you be partners in making sure the conversation stays on the track you agreed to. For example, after you agree on the purpose, you might say, "Let's agree on how we want to have the feedback. I'd like to share with you the specific examples where I think you have done well and the examples where I have concerns. For the concerns, if we agree on the examples, then we can figure out what led to things not going well, and jointly decide what needs to happen to improve. How does that sound to you? Anything about what I'm suggesting that you would like to change?"

Jointly design the order of the feedback. Many leaders assume that others want to receive feedback using the sandwich approach (start with some positive, then give the negative, then end on a positive note). They've been taught (erroneously) that the negative feedback goes down easier (and is easier for them) when it's sandwiched between slices of positive feedback. Rather than assume this, simply ask the person you're giving feedback to how they would like to receive it. You might say, "I don't have a preference for how I share the feedback. My interest is that you and I learn as much as possible about what will help improve your performance. I can start with the things you've done well or the things I'm concerned about. Or you can start. We can go chronologically through the year or any other way that makes sense. How you would you like to do it?" Again, when people jointly design the process, they have more commitment to it.

Give the headlines—don't make people guess. When you give negative feedback, state exactly what you've seen and what your concern is, then ask for the other person's point of view. You might say, "One of the places I think you slipped this year compared to last year is holding your people accountable. Let me give you a few examples and get your reactions." As a rule of thumb, if it takes more than two sentences for the person receiving feedback to know what your concern is, you're probably beating around the bush. You may be doing this to save face for you, the other person, or both. Unfortunately, it does what you want to avoid: making the other person more anxious and defensive.

Ask about your own contribution—before anyone else raises it. You work with people you give feedback to. That means your performance affects their performance just as theirs affects yours. It's not realistic to talk about your direct reports' performance without considering how you contribute to it. When you tell someone, "This conversation is about your performance, not mine," you're ignoring the reality of your working relationship, asking the person to be accountable for behavior without doing the same yourself, and you're controlling the conversation. That all makes people defensive. To be accountable, toward the beginning of the conversation say something like, "I'm open to the possibility that I may be contributing to the very things that I'm concerned about in your performance. If I am, I'd really like you to tell me."

> *It's not realistic to talk about your direct reports' performance without considering how you contribute to it.*

Don't worry that acknowledging your contribution means that the person is no longer accountable. Even if you have contributed to the problem, your direct report is still likely to have contributed, too.

If someone seems to get defensive—stay curious! You can't prevent people from getting defensive; you can only control your own behavior to reduce the chance that you contribute to their defensiveness. If someone does seem to get defensive, you can simply ask about it by saying, "I noticed in the last couple of minutes, you've gotten quiet—yes? I'm wondering, are you feeling like I'm putting you on the defensive?" If the person says yes, you can say something like, "I wasn't trying to make you feel that way, but I may have done something that I wasn't aware of. Is there anything that I've done that contributed to it?" It's amazing what you can learn when you're genuinely curious.

Hold others accountable—don't allow anonymous feedback. If you really want to frustrate someone and inspire a defensive reaction, talk about the concerns others have and then say you can't reveal who said it. Or worse, say something like, "It doesn't matter who said it; what's important is your performance." This is standard operating procedure for many organizations, even for cutting-edge ones that offer 360-degree feedback. If the purpose of performance feedback is to help someone develop, it's nearly impossible to achieve this without making it possible to talk with people directly about the actions that concern them. Of course, asking others to give feedback to their peers and bosses often requires a change in culture. But if you can't be accountable for giving others you work with feedback, your organization isn't likely to perform at a very high level.

If other team members want to give you feedback about Dahlia, remind them that each person is accountable for sharing their own information. Consider saying something like this:

> "I think that's important information for Dahlia to have so she can improve—what do you think? [If the complainer agrees, continue:] Because that happened with you and I wasn't present, that's your feedback to give. If you want help, I can help you prepare to give her the feedback. I can even be there with you when you give it, if you want. But I can't give it for you because that shifts the accountability from you to me. In addition, Dahlia is likely to have questions that I

won't be able to answer, and then the feedback won't be specific enough to enable her to change. Do you see any of this differently?"

If you don't share the negative feedback soon, don't impose penalties based on it. Negative feedback should have a statute of limitations. The longer you wait to give it, the longer you contribute to the person's ineffectiveness and the less time they have to improve. A good guideline is that unless you're giving someone feedback on something done in the few weeks before a review, if you haven't already shared the feedback, you shouldn't use it to reduce the person's performance rating. That's part of what it means to hold yourself accountable to those who report to you.

Get feedback on how you're giving feedback. Just as you want others to learn to improve their work performance, learn how to improve your efforts to develop others. Ask them what you did in the feedback session that was helpful and what they would like you to do differently next time. Then *you* can practice and model receiving feedback without getting defensive.

WORKING AS A TEAM WHEN YOU'RE NOT TOGETHER

These days, people often have to work as a team when they're out of one another's sight, whether down the hall or on the other side of the world. That means they constantly have to deal with talking about absent teammates, addressing disagreements they have with each other, and preventing end runs around each other.

Talking About Teammates Who Aren't Present

Recently I was working with a leadership team in which members talked about each other behind their backs. They acknowledged this habit was eroding trust and hindering the team's efforts to execute its organizational strategy. At one point a team member suggested that they should stop talking about each other behind their backs. I disagreed.

I suggested they continue to do so. In fact, I suggested that they were better served by talking about each other, whether a person was there or not. But they needed to change the way they talked.

The problem with talking about absent teammates is that the people you're talking to don't get to hear the views of the person you're talking about. Instead they hear only your views on the person—and sometimes those views are negative. If you have issues with an absent person, it may seem like an easy way to build your case with the people you're talking to, but it has unintended consequences. It erodes your relationship with the person you are talking about, it sends a message to others that this behavior is acceptable, and it leaves the people you're talking to wondering what you say about *them* when they aren't present. Here are guidelines you can use when talking about someone who isn't present:

Represent the person's views that you disagree with. If you want to be a leader who brings people together rather than creates divisiveness, tell the people you're talking with what the other person's views are. For example, after you have explained why you think it's important to speed up the product launch date, you might say, "Kay sees it differently. She wants to wait until Q3 to launch."

Remember, to represent Kay's views to others, you have to first talk with her directly. If you find yourself thinking, "I don't understand what her problem is," do some homework. Ask Kay not only what her view is, but how she came to that point of view. If you can't represent Kay's reasoning to others, then you probably can't fairly represent her views either.

Explain the source of your disagreement. It's even more helpful if you describe the cause of your different views. For example, you might say, "Kay and I have different assumptions about the timing of the launch and how it will affect our new products. She thinks if we speed up the launch date, we'll confuse customers with the products we launched last quarter. I think we'll actually speed up our new product line identity." Again, if you find yourself thinking, "I don't know why she disagrees with me," do some more homework. Talk with Kay.

Explain the person's views without making it an attack. Telling people that Kay doesn't understand the business, is generally clueless, or is out to make your part of the organization look bad only reinforces organizational silos. It's fine to say that you disagree and why you disagree, but don't do so by questioning her motives or simply dismissing her as clueless.

Give yourself the "Would They Consider It Fair?" test. You know you've done a good job of talking about Kay if, having heard what you said about her, she can say, "You've represented me accurately." So next time you're about to talk about someone you disagree with, first try this thought experiment. Listen to what you plan to say and ask yourself, "If the person heard what I am about to say, would she say I have represented her fairly?" If your answer is yes, you're leading by building better relationships. If the answer is no, what do you need to change to pass your test?

Preventing End Runs

As the team leader, you may be contributing unknowingly to your team members' acting unilaterally and making end runs around their teammates. If Lance comes to you saying, "I've got a problem with Sam" and you start to solve it, you've allowed Lance to shift the accountability for this problem from Sam and him to you. Even worse than solving the problem for Lance is agreeing to talk to Sam yourself. That completely shifts the accountability from Lance to you. Meanwhile, you don't have all the relevant information that Lance does, so you won't be able to answer Sam's questions—and so neither of you will be able to craft a solution based on informed choice.

Your first comment to Lance should be, "Have you talked with Sam about the fact that you've got a problem with him?" If the answer is no, your second question should be, "What's led you to not talk with him about it?"

It's important to tell Lance that you see your role as helping him develop the ability to work out these issues with other team members, not for you to work them out for him. It's fine to coach Lance on how he can productively talk and work with Sam. It's even reasonable for you to meet with Lance and Sam together and help them resolve their problem. But if you take on the role of solving problems for team members, your reward will be this: team members will give you more opportunities to solve their problems. That's a prescription for failing to develop team members' abilities, and for reducing the time you have to focus on other priorities.

When Direct Reports Can't Agree

What do your direct reports do when they need to agree on a decision, but can't? You've probably seen this situation. Two of your direct reports have strong views on a topic, the stakes are high for both of them, and they can't bridge the gap.

If they're using a unilateral control approach, they're each thinking they need to influence you so their own position wins out. They may try to get to your office before the other one does. Alternatively, if they think you're the "decides-based-on-the-last-person-who-got-a-word-in" type, they may try to figure out when you have talked with the other teammate so as to swoop in afterwards.

In any case, the problem with one person escalating the issue to you is that not all of the information gets on the table, which undermines commitment. You don't get to hear all the information and neither do the direct reports who are escalating the issue to you. When one direct report finds out that the other has prevailed with you, both will have a larger problem to solve—they will lose trust in each other.

As the leader of the team, you can ask your direct reports to be accountable to each other, not just to you. If you're using the mutual learning approach, you're thinking that you want everyone to be transparent and to accept accountability, and you want to ensure that everyone can make an informed choice. Ask them to jointly design a way to bring their disagreement to you. When direct reports are in conflict with each other and at an impasse, have them come to you together. The first direct report to recognize that they are at an impasse might say to the other,

"I think we've gone as far as we can by ourselves and we still don't have a decision that we can both support. Do you see that the same way? If you agree that we're stuck, I suggest we go together to [your name here], describe where we are, and figure out the next step together. I want to make sure [name] hears each of our views, so we all hear the same thing at the same time and we're all involved in the next step. How does that sound?"

Before they get to a meeting with you, ask them to prepare together as follows:

1. *Identify the source of their disagreement.* Is it that they disagree about some information? Is it that they have different needs that they can't reconcile? Or is it that they are making different assumptions that lead them to different conclusions?

2. *List the possible solutions that the two of them have considered.* Ask them to be ready to explain what it is about each of their solutions that didn't work for the other.

3. *Be ready to tell you what they need from you to help resolve the disagreement.* Do they need you to validate whose assumptions are correct? Do they need you to identify which of the competing interests should take priority?

By asking your direct reports to jointly design a way to resolve their disagreements, you increase the chance of a high-quality decision with high commitment that maintains or improves your working relationships. And you ensure that your reports do not inappropriately depend on you.

USING MUTUAL LEARNING IN E-MAIL

E-mail may be your main mode of business communication and problem solving. You can apply the same core values and behaviors in e-mail that you use in face-to-face and phone interactions. Here are some tips for making your e-mail communication much more effective:

- Explain your reasoning.
- Share your views and ask genuine questions.
- Test your assumptions and inferences.
- Name your feelings—don't let people guess them.
- Stop typing, start phoning.

Explain your reasoning. Just as you explain your reasoning in face-to-face conversation, so you can do in e-mail. As I was writing this paragraph I received e-mail from a colleague who asked, "Will you need me on this client engagement in March?" She then explained (I'm paraphrasing), "I can't find any information saying whether this project work has been confirmed. Another client wants me to work on these dates. My preference is to do the engagement with you; I'm not trying to get out of it." By explaining why she was asking, my colleague gave me all the information I needed not only to answer her question but to avoid wrong inferences about why she was asking. I can now give her an answer that speaks directly to her needs. Add the extra sentence or two that are needed to explain your reasoning whether you're asking a question, sharing a decision, or taking an action. It saves time and frustration.

Share your views and ask genuine questions. When you send e-mail, don't simply state your views; follow them by asking a genuine question to learn. Instead of simply writing, "I think we should have the meeting off-site so we don't get people drifting in and out," continue by writing something like, "What problems, if any, do you think this would create?" By getting curious and asking a genuine question, you increase the chance that when people respond, they will be addressing your question and you will be crafting a solution that takes into account the range of stakeholders needs.

Test your assumptions and inferences. The same sorts of assumptions and inferences creep into e-mail as into phone or in-person conversations. And acting on ones that aren't true can easily cause problems. The first step is to become aware of the assumptions and inferences you're making by applying the ladder of inference method from Chapter Five. Read through each e-mail message before you send it, carefully looking for assumptions and inferences you are making. Acknowledge them for what they are. For example: "I think we absolutely need to resolve this issue for the client before next Tuesday. I'm setting this as the deadline because I'm assuming that we are still planning to meet with the client next Tuesday and I want the issue resolved before we all get together. Is my assumption still correct?"

Name your feelings—don't let people guess them. One problem with e-mail is that the reader can't hear your tone of voice, see your facial expressions, or watch your other nonverbal behavior. That means that sometimes the reader can't easily tell whether your "I think this project took a lot of your work and didn't bear the fruit we expected" is one of compassion, frustration, or something else. It's particularly frustrating when your intent was to be compassionate and the reader interprets you as complaining or being annoyed. Don't make someone guess. Tell the reader what you're feeling. Write something like, "I'm not frustrated with you about this, I'm concerned that others didn't share information with you that would have helped you better navigate the project." If you're frustrated, say so and explain why.

Stop typing, start phoning. We have so many text-based ways of miscommunicating with each other: mobile phones, Skyping, texting, standard e-mail, and doubtless others now being invented. I've noticed that messages I send from my iPhone are shorter—and explain less—than messages I send from my laptop or desktop computer. It takes me more effort to type on my small iPhone keyboard than on my laptop. I've noticed the same pattern for those who send me e-mail. But some messages aren't meant for e-mail in any case. When you're dealing with an issue that involves testing a number of assumptions, explaining much of your reasoning or asking others about their reasoning, or talking about feelings, stop typing and pick up the phone. It's much more interactive, so you can better explain your views and understand others—in less time than it would take to swap multiple e-mails.

A QUALIFICATION TO "SPEAKING WITH ONE VOICE" AS A TEAM

Leadership teams often have a rule that after they reach a decision, they speak with one voice. Once they leave the room, each team member is expected to fully support the team decision. Any concerns expressed in the room remain in the room, not to be shared with team members' direct reports.

There's nothing wrong with expecting that after the team reaches a decision everyone will support it. But requiring team members to leave their concerns inside the team room creates problems rather than solves them. When your team members talk to their direct reports about implementing the decision, the direct reports are likely to have concerns. It's also likely that the direct reports will have expressed their concerns to their leader (your leadership team members) before your leadership team made the decision and that the leader had expressed some of the same concerns in those discussions.

So put yourself in their shoes and imagine telling your own direct reports that you now fully support a higher-level team decision. What do you say when someone asks, "What about the problems that we talked with you about?" Whether you now deny you ever thought there were problems or you don't address the concerns, you have two problems: you'll find it hard to implement the decision with the direct reports who had concerns, and it's likely you'll lose credibility with those direct reports.

Mutual learning teams expect that when the team makes a decision, everyone agrees to support it through their actions and their voices. Mutual learning teams also encourage members to share their concerns with their direct reports. If you don't share your concerns, you're not transparent. So team members are free to discuss the concerns that they had going into the leadership team meeting and the concerns that they still have after the decision—as long as they make it clear that, having heard the information and interests of others, they are supporting the decision and expect their direct reports to do so as well.

Mutual learning teams expect that when the team makes a decision, everyone agrees to support it through their actions and their voices. Mutual learning teams also encourage members to share their concerns with their direct reports.

HELPING YOUR TEAM INFLUENCE YOU

Your direct reports spend a lot of time thinking how best to influence you. You probably spend time listening to them try to influence you. You can save them and yourself time and effort simply by telling them what it will take to influence you.

There are times when you'll be making a decision for the team after getting input from team members. Although you haven't made a decision, you've thought about the issue and realize that only certain kinds of information will influence your decision.

Tell people what kind of information will influence you. You might say, "I'm leaning toward combining the two groups instead of keeping them separate. I'm convinced it makes sense in terms of reliability and cost. I think it also makes sense for improving service quality, but I'm not completely sure. I'm open to being influenced about that. If you have information or thoughts about how it will affect service quality, I'm open to hearing that."

If you were operating from a unilateral control mindset, this strategy wouldn't make any sense. Telling people how to influence you is like helping others beat you. But in mutual learning, it's simply being transparent about your reasoning. This helps others be accountable for the kind of information they share with you so that you can make a more informed choice. It also saves time.

Team members can use a similar approach with you or anyone else they want to influence. Rather than trying to figure out whether someone is open to being influenced, they simply ask something like, "Are you open to being influenced on this issue? I'm asking because I don't want to take your time or my time if you're not." If you say you're still open to being influenced, the team member could ask you, "What would influence you? What kind of information would make a difference for you? I'm asking because it will help me quickly figure out if I have some information that could be useful to you." By being curious, the team member asks you to be transparent and account-able. That enables both of you to make a more informed choice.

CHAPTER 8

Becoming a Smarter Leader

To address the natural gap between learning about a concept and applying that concept in real life, this chapter provides some practical advice on making the mutual learning mindset your own and building effective behaviors based on it. You may find it useful to slip bookmarks into the pages with Figures 3.4 (The Virtuous Cycle of Mutual Learning) and 6.1 (Team Effectiveness Model) to make it easy to refer to them as ongoing guides.

BEGINNING THE JOURNEY

If you routinely set goals and achieve them, or at least come close, the broad sequence suggested here should fit your style. First take stock of where you are and where you'd like to be. From that, develop an action plan. Once these things are reasonably clear, talk with your team about what you are doing. As that conversation develops, jointly plan with the team members how they will support your personal progress.

Take Stock

As part of taking stock, compare your current results, behaviors, and mindset with the results, behaviors, and mindset you want. Also increase your awareness of situations that trigger you to shift into patterns of mutual learning or unilateral control.

Comparisons

In your comparisons, begin with results—the ones you want to achieve versus those you presently get. From results, work back to behaviors and mindsets.

The results to consider here are the ones you want to achieve for yourself, not results for the team as a whole. For example, are you trying to make better personal decisions? Trying to reduce implementation time for the things you do that don't depend on the team as a whole? Trying to build your own personal trust with others? Compare each of these desired results with the results you're actually getting.

Next, move to behaviors, including the eight described in Chapter Four and Chapter Five and others that may be important to you. Look over each current result and identify the actual behaviors that you've employed in reaching it. Work through some specific examples. For instance, if you're trying to make better decisions with others, think about some group decisions that were disappointing or frustrating for you. Reviewing them through the lens of unilateral control, what *behaviors* led you to get those results? Were you stating your views and not asking others for their views? Were you focused on your position? Were you making assumptions that you didn't test and that turned out be wrong? If you find yourself focusing on others' ineffective behaviors, refocus by asking yourself, "How did I respond to those behaviors ineffectively?"

When you identify the unilateral control behaviors that led to these results, you'll also be able to recognize mutual learning behaviors that can lead you to the results you want. In this case, you would want to work on stating your views and asking genuine questions, focusing on interests instead of positions, and testing assumptions and inferences.

Next, from behaviors, work back to mindset. Again, by spotting what values and assumptions were operating in ineffective examples, you'll be able to recognize different ones that will support more effective behaviors. Of course, the mutual learning approach and the unilateral control approach are systems, so all the core values and assumptions in each approach work together to help you create the behaviors that get your results.

But you'll discover that, for you, certain alternative values and assumptions are more challenging than others. Were you assuming that you understood the situation and that others who disagreed with you didn't? Were you trying to win rather than to understand others? Then what mutual learning core values and assumptions would lead to the behaviors you wanted? For example, you may decide that what you need to do most is increase curiosity as one of your values and more often assume that you might be missing things that others are picking up on.

Review the mutual learning assessment identified in Chapter One, and take it again—or take it now if you didn't before. Now that you have a better sense of the mutual learning mindset and behaviors, you can get a more accurate assessment of how you stand in relation to them.

When you finish this process for one problematic situation, you will have identified key elements of the mutual learning mindset and behaviors that you want to adopt. If you repeat the process for other situations in which you feel your results fell short, you'll notice the same patterns of behaviors, core values, and assumptions. The truth is, how we do one thing is pretty much how we do other things, too. Start to change those elements of your mindset and behaviors and you will reap the benefits in many situations.

Triggers

In taking stock, also identify triggers that lead you into either one mindset or the other. In any given situation, you have a choice about what mindset to maintain, though you may not recognize the possibility. If you identify in advance what triggers propel you into a unilateral control mindset, you can become aware of that in the moment of challenge and choose a mutual learning approach instead.

Think about situations in which you acted from a unilateral control mindset. What triggered that frame of mind? As I said earlier, people generally use a unilateral control approach when they feel challenged, threatened, or embarrassed in some way. The stakes might be particularly high for you, you might be overly invested in your own idea for a solution, or you might be responding to someone else's unilateral behavior.

If you can't remember what has triggered you in the past, start to notice the next few times you end up in unilateral control. These will also be great moments to ask for feedback from others. Almost certainly, the people on whom you're using it will see it clearly and may also have ideas about what set you off in that direction. This will be valuable information later, as well, when you talk with your team about how to support your change in leadership.

Develop a Personal Action Plan

Having taken stock of new values and assumptions you want to use and the broad behaviors that stem from them, begin three planning steps: choose the contexts in which you will begin to apply your new approach; set goals of personal change; and schedule time for continued planning, self-assessment, and feedback.

Choose the Contexts

Will you first try out your personal changes only with your team of direct reports? How about with your peers? With your boss? With clients, customers, or vendors? The more variety in the people with whom you try it, the better your ultimate results will be in each case. Also, the more often you use the approach, the sooner you will start to get the results you're trying to achieve.

You have lots of chances to practice, whenever others are around. One of my pet peeves is working with leaders who say, "Roger, I haven't had much chance to practice my mutual learning approach in the past few weeks." Unless you're stuck in a closet, you have lots of chances to practice. (OK, maybe I could use some more compassion here.) Even small, commonplace interactions—a brief exchange with a staff member or assistant at work, with a cashier where you shop, a waiter where you dine, or elsewhere is an opportunity to practice transparency, curiosity, and more. By practicing in simple encounters first, you increase your ability to handle weightier moments as well.

If you practice the approach at home, here's a tip for domestic harmony: Tell your spouse or partner or child that you've figured out how *you've* been contributing to the challenges in the relationship, and you'll be welcomed for your new insights—however overdue— and commitment to improving the relationship. That works much better than saying you've figured out how your family has fallen short. Also keep in mind that this is about *your* practice, not what others may need to do.

Set Goals for Personal Change

Trite but true, no matter what behaviors you're trying to change, setting specific goals increases the chance that you will create the change you want. Publicly telling others your goals also enables others to help you achieve them.

From what you discovered while taking stock, besides setting overall goals for performance, working relationships, and your well-being, note outcomes you want to achieve when working with particular individuals or groups and set goals for specific meetings, conversations, e-mail exchanges, and decisions. For example, for meetings with your direct reports, you may want to set a goal of being curious enough to understand their assumptions and interests, and the relevant information they have about the situation. For the same interaction, you might also want to set a goal of being transparent about these things yourself.

Forget silver bullets. You'll never find one thing to say or do, one line to write, or one decision to make that will magically create greater performance, stronger working relationships, or increased well-being. Still, don't underestimate the power of each interaction to improve the dynamic between you and those you work with.

Schedule Ongoing Planning, Self-Assessment, and Feedback

Systematic change rises out of cycles of planning, acting, and reviewing. With your goals in mind, decide how you will set aside times and places for planning your actions, reviewing them, and getting feedback from others.

One leader I worked with set a time and place every morning, before he entered his office, to review his upcoming schedule and prepare for meetings or phone calls that might be challenging. He knew that once he was in the office, he'd have trouble reserving time to plan, even if he stopped all calls and closed his door. He could rarely plan immediately before meetings because they were often back-to-back. So he found a quiet out-of-the-way spot in his office skyscraper to sit with his morning coffee and review his upcoming day. For each meeting he identified what key elements of the mutual learning approach he needed to focus on and how he would choose to respond in situations he knew were likely to trigger him into unilateral control. He told me that these ten minutes of sheltered planning set him up for success the whole day. On those days that he didn't take the time to plan, he found himself getting stuck more, with poorer results.

Whether you plan for tomorrow's encounters tonight or at the start of the day at your desk or in some other spot in the morning, develop some habit for planning how you will apply mutual learning to upcoming scheduled interactions. Also set aside times for self-assessment and review previous decisions, interactions, and feedback, whether they were planned or spontaneous. This will help you make course corrections as you plan future meetings, e-mail exchanges, and so forth. The half-life of memory for meetings can be pretty short, so the sooner you review how each one went, the better.

Your self-assessment can be simple: compare your goals with what you actually achieved, then—whatever the outcome—compare the behaviors and the elements of the mindset you planned to use with the ones you actually used. Where you see gaps, ask yourself what happened that triggered you into a unilateral control mindset. Then, for next time, plan a different mental response.

As part of reviewing your interactions, plan when, how, and from whom you want feedback.

TALK WITH YOUR TEAM ABOUT WHAT YOU ARE DOING

Take some time to prepare how you will introduce mutual learning to your team—what to say and how to model it. Start out by clearly stating your purpose for the conversation. Let your team know that you plan to make changes in your way of leadership and want to get their reactions to your plan as well as ongoing feedback. (The discussion of Behavior 2 in Chapter Four includes a number of suggestions that would be useful here.) To summarize: Get right to it. Don't bury your lead or ease into the topic. The longer you take to declare your agenda, the more anxious team members will get as they tell themselves stories about what you're really up to. I guarantee they will be at least very curious—and perhaps concerned or relieved—about changes you plan to make in your leadership.

"Show and Tell" or Only "Show"?

How much should you say while you're changing your leadership approach? Should you just let your behavior speak for itself or should you also let people know exactly what you're up to? What will you tell them and when? What do you need to hear from them?

If you're using this new approach with people who have little prior relationship with you, you don't need to explain what's changed because they don't know how you were before. But in ongoing working relationships, it's important to explain that you're trying a change because people do make meaning in a way that reinforces their previous inferences. If your team members know you to have been unilaterally controlling at times and you simply start using a mutual learning approach, they may easily infer that you've found a new, more sophisticated way to control them. By explaining your new behavior and your intent, you'll increase the chance that they will make the meaning of your new behavior that you hope they'll make. You'll also get more and better (more specific) feedback because they'll understand your intent.

> *By explaining your new behavior and your intent, you'll increase the chance that they will make the meaning of your new behavior that you hope they'll make.*

Above all, introduce the mutual learning approach to your team by using it yourself even as you begin to talk about it. Nothing speaks louder and more credibly than your behavior. It lets others quickly see what you are talking about and how you want to act. Be prepared to model and to "be the change you want to see."

Explain Your Reasoning and Intent

As soon as you say that you want to change how you lead, team members will wonder why: "What's happened to him?" "Who's she been talking to?" "What's he been reading?" They'll think this even if they already agree you need to change. Be transparent about the various factors that have brought you to this point.

Your team will also wonder what your end goal is. Are you changing how you lead simply because you need to be more effective or are you changing how you lead because you think the entire team needs to be more effective? If you believe and say that the entire team needs to be more effective, be prepared for them to ask you why you aren't asking them to change right now as well. It's important to answer these questions. Even better is to anticipate their questions before they ask them. In the spirit of mutual learning, you might say: "I'm thinking you're wondering what my end goal is here and why I'm not asking you to change. Is anyone wondering that?"

When you say something like this you model how to raise an issue that the team might have thought was undiscussable. When you answer the question, hopefully with compassion, you model transparency, curiosity, and accountability, too.

Since you've decided to move yourself toward mutual learning leadership, you may also want your team to move there as well. Still, there are good reasons for changing yourself before you ask your team to do likewise. The modeling is one good reason, and going first can be especially useful if the change will be big and seems difficult for your team to understand.

Whatever your reasons, share and test them with the team. If you plan to model the approach so that you can later ask your team to adopt it, say that. If you're going it alone based on some inferences you've made about the team, be sure to test those inferences. Does the team need more information to make an informed choice? Do people really need to see that you're committed before they'll willingly commit? Test those inferences, and make it clear that's what you're doing. You may learn that the team is already willing to begin to change with you. You may also learn that team members need something else from you before they can commit to the change.

Also model the mutual learning assumption that you realize you may be contributing to the problem. Give specific examples of how your leadership has contributed to low team performance and challenging working relationships. Team members will quickly notice your willingness to be transparent and make yourself vulnerable about your own leadership in the team. That will make it easier for them to share their own thoughts about your contributions. You might say something like this:

> "From reading and thinking, I've realized there are a number of things I do that can undercut the quality of our decision making. For example, when I've got a solution in mind, I tend to propose it and push for buy-in without finding out what kinds of problems the solution might create for each of you. As a result, we end up going with a solution that creates problems for some of you, and then I get frustrated with you because of those problems. For example, last month when we were deciding whether to outsource part of IT, I pushed for a solution to outsource, even though Brent, Suzanne, and Kate all said it would slow our response time. Instead of getting curious and understanding how you thought that would happen, I pushed ahead. Now we're already hearing that response time is stretching out. How does that fit with your understanding of what happened?"

Also go on to explain how you would handle the situation differently. Providing a before-and-after contrast makes it easier for your team to understand how you will change and what to expect. And it enables you to hear their reactions. For example, you might say:

> "If I were making the decision about IT today, I would do it differently. I would still share my view about the solution I proposed, but I would explain more about how I thought the solution met each of our needs as well as the larger organization's needs. Then I would have been curious. I'd ask you, 'Am I correctly describing your needs or am I off somewhere?' I'm thinking if I did that, you would have said more clearly what needs my solution didn't meet. Then I would have asked us to craft a solution that met all the needs we had identified. If I'd done that, I'm guessing we would have made a better decision and that neither you nor I would be as frustrated now. What are your reactions to how I would handle the situation now?"

As you describe the purpose of the meeting, what changes you want to make, and the gaps you see, stop each time and get curious. Ask team members how they see the situation—both things about which they agree and things they see in a different light. This will help you avoid moving ahead without them. Take time to understand how they are thinking and to explore their questions. Do they agree with your examples? Do they see other examples of how you could lead more effectively?

Naturally, explaining your intent also includes explaining what you mean by "mutual learning." How much the team learns about it up front is up to you and them. There isn't one right way to introduce it, but in addition to giving specific examples that illustrate the difference between the unilateral control and mutual learning approaches, here are some key points to explain in your initial introduction:

- All of us have an operating system—a mindset—in our brain that drives our behavior. We are usually unaware of our mindset.
- Our mindset leads to our behavior, which leads to the results we get.
- There are basically two mindsets that people use to drive their behavior—unilateral control and mutual learning.
- In challenging situations almost all of us use a unilateral control mindset, and it gets us the results we are trying to avoid.
- Becoming a more effective leader means changing not only our behavior but the mindset that drives it. This takes practice and feedback from others.

You can expand on these key points by explaining the difference between unilateral control and mutual learning core values, assumptions, and behaviors, as well as the results that they create. Again, combine your explanations with curiosity by inviting questions and reactions. This will naturally lead you to share more of the information that you team needs.

After an initial introduction, you and your team can jointly design any additional steps so the team can learn more about the approach. Some options include reading this book or the article

"Eight Behaviors for Smarter Teams" (available at www.schwarz associates.com); asking team members to take the online mutual learning survey mentioned in Chapter One; and discussing the mutual learning core values, assumptions, and behaviors.

In all this, speak as much as you can in your own voice and language. I've written this book in my voice and used the terms I use when I work with leaders. But you don't need to sound like me. For example, if the word *inference* doesn't feel right to you, using it may make the team wonder whether you're sincere. In that case, instead of saying "I'm inferring," say "I'm thinking" or "It sounds to me" or any other phrase that sounds like you. Play with the mutual learning language until you land on words that work for you at whatever stage you're in.

Discuss How Your Changing Will Affect the Team

If you don't want to ask team members to start their own journeys with you right away, there's more you'll need to clarify, because you and your team are a system. Any changes in your own mindset and behavior will still have an impact on them. As you start to become more curious, you'll be asking them to share information that they may not have shared before. As you start to give the team more informed choice, they may need to ask more questions than they asked before and have greater involvement in some decisions. If you start to hold team members more accountable or be more accountable to the team, they may need to challenge others more—including you. Changing yourself is one way that you begin to change a system. If you change your leadership and don't expect that your team members' behavior will change at all, you're not making much change.

So when team members ask if they will need to change, be clear. Distinguish between the kind of change that comes from responding to your changes in behavior as opposed to the kind of change that would come if you were asking them to apply the mutual learning approach and take initiative in implementing it.

Develop Team Support Through Feedback

To develop your mutual learning mindset and skill set, you need to regularly practice giving feedback and getting it from your team. As you jointly design a way to do this, both you and your team need to consider how and when to give feedback, and also how to make feedback safe to give.

The more your team understands what your desired change will look like, the better feedback they can give you. For each of the changes you want to make, give your team an example of what the unilateral control behavior looks like and what the new mutual learning behavior looks like. You can also describe how you expect team members will feel if you create the change. Solicit feedback at useful moments. For example, you might say:

> "One of the changes I want to make is shifting from thinking 'I'm right, you're wrong' to thinking that 'each of us sees things others don't.' As part of that change, I plan to replace my leading rhetorical questions with genuine ones. So, when one of you proposes a solution that makes no sense to me, instead of saying, 'Are you out of your mind?' I may say something like, 'I just don't see your proposal as a solution. Can you tell me how it will address the root causes of the problem?' I'm not simply changing my words; I really am curious. So instead of your feeling like I'm putting you down or shutting you down, I'm hoping you'll feel engaged because I'm genuinely interested in your thinking. Bottom line, we should get more of the information on the table and make better decisions. What questions or thoughts do you have about this change I want to make—the shift away from 'I'm right, you're wrong'?"

Remember that your mindset affects your behavior in general, not just your spoken words. The decisions you make, the process you use for making them, the e-mail you send, and all the other ways you take action—all these can be subjects for feedback on how you're applying mutual learning. The broader the range of actions on which your team can give you feedback, the more powerful the feedback can be. Besides negative feedback, emphasize that you also want your team be willing to give you positive feedback when you're successfully making the changes you said you want to make. This will reinforce the change and can be motivating.

After the team understands how you want to change, you'll want to agree on when they can best give you ongoing feedback to support your change. The prompter the feedback, the more useful it will be, and the sooner you can apply it. It's most helpful to get feedback in the same setting and time that your behavior occurred. If you're in a meeting with your team and aren't explaining your reasoning, it's most effective for a team member to give you the feedback as it happens. This enables other team members to say whether they saw your behavior the same way or differently. It also enables you to make any corrections in the moment and avoid or reduce any negative consequences that might have stemmed from your unilateral control behavior.

The more you're willing to accept feedback in the moment, the more you model the value of learning promptly from and with others. But there may be times when you prefer that others not give you feedback in the moment. You may feel that some moments and settings are too vulnerable or otherwise inappropriate as times for you to receive it. For example, are you willing to get feedback from your team members in front of your boss? Your peers? How about in front of customers?

Also work out with them *how* they can best give you feedback. In the ideal world, people would give you feedback using the method for testing inferences that I described in Chapter Five. In short, they would describe what they heard you say or do, check to see if you hear it the same way, and then describe how they saw it as consistent or inconsistent with what you said you wanted to change, checking again with you. You can talk with your team about what would make the most useful feedback for you. But keep in mind that doing so takes them further down the path of learning the mutual learning approach—a path they may not be ready to travel. So, in any case, be prepared to get feedback in which team members make statements and don't check to see whether you agree, and make untested inferences about what you were trying to do. When you receive feedback that seems unilaterally controlling, your challenge will be to respond from a mutual learning mindset.

Safety matters. You'll get better feedback if you make it safe for your team to give it.[1] This means creating an environment in which they can communicate to you without being embarrassed, belittled, or punished. The paradox here is that this safe environment may be something you're still in the process of trying to create, based on a mutual learning mindset, so team members may not routinely feel safe about bringing up feedback, especially about whether they feel safe. Some may give you feedback, even so, even when you lapse into a unilateral control approach. But by and large, if you respond to team member feedback by getting defensive—arguing about the feedback, shutting down the conversation, or even retaliating—team members will infer you're not genuinely interested and will stop giving you feedback or give less frequent and less honest feedback. You will have undermined your own broader ability to learn from your team.

Ask your team what they would need in order to give you specific and honest feedback. Then listen carefully and jointly design ways to create those conditions. One way to make it easier for you to recognize and prepare when team members are giving feedback is to have them use some obvious, agreed-upon, prefacing phrase. It might be as simple as, "Can I give you some feedback now?" It's also useful to have an agreed-upon phrase by which they can prime you for the news that you seem to be responding defensively to the feedback.

Ask your team what they would need in order to give you specific and honest feedback. Then listen carefully and jointly design ways to create those conditions.

That's important because your defensiveness may tend to block out negative feedback.

CONTINUING YOUR PERSONAL PROGRESS

You can start out quickly, seeing some results when you first make changes, but the more steadily you practice, the more you'll be able to spontaneously handle increasingly challenging situations with self-confidence. You'll find that as you get better at using mutual learning, you see additional changes you can make to further improve your results. Over time you'll get to the point where, in most situations, you use a mutual learning approach without having to actively think about it.

As in any significant journey of change, expect some setbacks. You will still have days when meetings and conversations don't go well. You'll send e-mail that turns people off. You'll make decisions unilaterally that would have been better if you had approached them with a mutual learning mindset. The important thing is to analyze and get feedback on the situations in which you weren't as effective as you wanted to be and continue applying the approach. It's also important to acknowledge and celebrate your successes along the way. You will have earned it.

Becoming a Smarter Team

Getting your entire team to use a mutual learning approach is much more powerful than changing your own approach alone. As a team you can learn faster and achieve better results quicker. You can give one another better support as you change. But there's a more basic reason for changing as a team. If you read this book because you wanted better results from your team, ultimately you and your team will need to change. In this chapter I describe the steps to take if you and your team want to start this journey together or if, after seeing you work on your own, your team members are ready to join you.

For best results, your team members need to make an informed choice to change their approach. In practice, that means talking with your team about the mutual learning approach and what using it looks like, and asking them to experiment with it for a while before making a decision about whether to adopt it.

Remember, you're raising the stakes when you propose team change or even asking team members to experiment with mutual learning, and your team will know it: you're asking *them* to make fundamental changes. The stakes being higher, the task will require greater commitment from them. So team members are likely to have a lot more concerns. When you described your plan to change only your approach, they were probably somewhat interested in your assessment of the team. Now they will have many more questions about why you're calling for wider change, whether you see the team as ineffective or dysfunctional, and the extent to which they really have a team at all.

So expect a longer, wider-ranging, and less predictable conversation—something the group won't be able to complete in a single two-hour leadership team meeting. The meetings will also be more challenging for you to manage. Expect the conversation to be less linear as team members share critical thoughts, raising unanticipated questions and concerns that need to be answered in the process of building commitment. Expect team members to ask for examples of what you have seen in the team that leads you to propose this change; take time before meetings to come up with examples. As team members raise more challenging questions and issues, including ones that to you seem initially off-topic, it will be both important and difficult to respond with genuine curiosity and without getting defensive.

BEGINNING THE TEAM JOURNEY

Beginning to develop a smarter team follows much the same path as beginning to change your own mindset and approach, from taking stock through engaging the team and onward through joint planning.

Taking Private Stock Again

Once again, begin by yourself, privately taking stock of your team, comparing its current results with results you'd like it to achieve, then moving back to team design (context, structure, and process) including behaviors, and finally to mindset. As you do this, also gather your observations and thoughts about where individual members of the team may be in terms of mutual learning.

As part of taking stock, identify the mindset elements that you believe will lead to the effective team context, structure, and process, as well as desirable team behaviors, and compare them to the current mindset elements that you think the team and individual members are using. Be aware here, as you dip below observable team results, structures, process, and behaviors, you are only tentatively identifying the core values and assumptions that others are using. You can't directly observe someone's mindset, so you're making inferences and attributions about what your team members are thinking. You'll need to test these inferences and attributions later as you discuss them with the team. You may also want to share with the team your assessment of your own mindset.

Consider results related to performance, working relationships, and individual well-being. Consider results that you identified as you've read through the book. Does the team need to be more innovative? Reduce costs? Manage conflict more effectively? Lower the level of stress? The more specific you can be about results, the better the team will be able to understand. Do you have data that speaks to the results? Stories that will bring the issue to life for the team? When you finish taking stock of results, you should have lists of specific results the team needs as well as results it is currently getting, along with data and illustrative anecdotes.

For example, if you're trying to make better decisions in the team, think about some decisions that were disappointing or frustrating for you. Reviewing them through the lens of the unilateral control approach, what behaviors led the team to get those results? Your work to identify your own unilateral control behaviors in the team will be an important first step here. Now consider how other members may be acting in similar ways.

When you finish taking private stock of the team, you will have created a story of the results that the team needs and how it can achieve them as well as a contrasting story of the team's current results and the causes. These two stories will be a central part of the conversation with your team. But these are only your stories and they are incomplete. Treat them as hypotheses for your team to jointly test and modify—if they're yours and you win by getting the team to adopt them, you're back in the arms of unilateral control.

Beginning to Talk with the Team

When you're ready to plan your first talk with the team, keep in mind the same basic considerations that matter when approaching them about your individual change. For example, you don't want to bury the lead or delay telling everyone that the meeting is about your desire that the entire team work toward more effective mutual learning. Don't ease in by saying you simply want to try some new behaviors. At the same time, be clear that before a decision is reached about whether the team should adopt the approach, you want to give team members the information and experience they need to make an informed choice.

Prepare specific examples of your own progress and of how you yourself still also need to change. Plan to state that you're open to being influenced and that you want every team member to be giving feedback to all members of the team. You'll need to let the group know you want a conversation in which each of you learns from and with all the others about the state of the team.

Plan to model a mutual learning approach. Start off again with why you want the whole team to discuss whether to pursue a mutual learning approach. Admit you could be wrong about what you're proposing and that you trust the wisdom of the mutual learning process and team to test whether or not to proceed. Your opening might sound something like this:

"I have three goals for our meeting. First, I want to talk with you about changes I've been trying to make in my leadership approach, including what's led me to want to make these changes, and get your reactions. Second, I want to talk with you about changes that I'd like our entire team to make in how we work together as a team. I think we can get better results as a team. I want to share my thinking about this and hear your thinking. I want to be clear: I'm not saying that I've already decided that the team will adopt the approach. I want us to learn more about the approach and experiment with it for a while before we make that decision. That brings me to my third goal for the meeting. I'd like for us to come to agreement about how we can learn enough about the mutual approach and experiment with it to make an informed choice about whether it's a good fit for us. I'm thinking that this conversation will probably take more than one meeting. It's an important topic for us and I want to give it the time it deserves. Given the goals I've described, does anyone have other related goals you want to add to the agenda?"

If you've concluded that you want the team to get involved in changing at the same moment that you're starting, you might say something like:

"I've thought about whether to start first by changing only myself and then later asking you as a team to change. But on balance, I think it would be easier, quicker, and more productive if we change as a team. Learning with and from each other is at the heart of the mutual learning approach. The sooner we begin the journey as a team, the sooner we'll start to reap the benefits for ourselves and the organization. What questions and thoughts do you have about what I'm suggesting?"

About your modeling, you might tell them:

"I'll be trying to use the mutual learning approach in our meeting today. I'll also try to point out how I'm using the approach as I'm using it. Keep in mind, I'm just learning to use this approach myself. I'm not very good at it yet. Don't expect that I'll be anything close to a model of mutual learning. If I say or do something you have questions about, just ask me. It will be a good way to understand more about the approach."

Be prepared for the question, "What's wrong with our team? Don't you think we're effective?" If you're fortunate, team members will ask it directly. (If you're really fortunate, they'll ask it in a genuinely curious form.) In case they don't ask it, be prepared to raise and answer it yourself. You might say something like:

> "I said earlier that I thought we could be more effective as a team. I don't think our team is broken. I think we do some things very well as a team, but I think we get stuck a fair amount and we really need to improve on some things. Let me give you a couple of examples and get your reactions. [Do so.] One reason I want to have this conversation is that I'm interested in our discussing how we are effective and how we can improve. One of my goals for this conversation is to begin to develop a common understanding about this."

Prepare examples of current team results that seem unsatisfactory to you so you'll be able to test whether team members really agree with your evaluation, and with your belief that the unilateral control approach is a significant contributing factor and that more mutual learning is likely to bring about worthwhile change.

Help team members understand the key points about team effectiveness (see Chapter Six for more detail):

- Team effectiveness starts with the mutual learning mindset and ends with mutual learning results. Like the mutual learning approach, how the team thinks affects how it works together and the results it gets.
- Team design is essential for creating strong team results. Here too, the mindset that leaders use to design the team affects the team results.
- The eight behaviors (described in Chapters Four and Five and incorporated under Structures in Figure 6.1) are ways to put the mutual learning mindset into action.

It's important that team members understand what becoming a mutual learning team will look like. It's not intuitively obvious to most. When your entire team uses the mutual learning approach, it changes the nature of leadership in the team, moving—as I said in Chapter One—from one-leader-in-the-room to a shared leadership approach. Because members may differ in what they understand by "shared leadership," be sure to say what you do and don't mean by it and to reach a shared definition. Table 9.1 answers questions about the two approaches and may help you talk with the team about first experimenting with the approach and then later deciding whether to adopt it.

If your team prefers to read about a topic before discussing it, you might refer them to selected parts of this book or the article "Eight Behaviors for Smarter Teams" (available at www.schwarz associates.com). Of course, you and your team can jointly design other ways for them to learn more about the approach.

When your entire team uses the mutual learning approach, it changes the nature of leadership in the team, moving from one-leader-in-the-room to a shared leadership approach.

In this team-change conversation, you may also want to give or even ask for examples of how other team members seemed to contribute to less-than-expected performance and working relationships. If your team has never had a conversation like this, the members may not be ready for this level of risk. So, jointly design with them whether they are willing to have that conversation. But even if the team is willing, begin with yourself. Model your own new assumption—"I may be contributing to the problem"—by giving specific examples of your own past contributions to less-than-expected results or relationships, along with how you want to think and act now and in the future. Then solicit the team's reactions.

Table 9.1. Comparing Unilateral Control and Mutual Learning Approaches to Leadership in Teams

	Unilateral Control	**Mutual Learning**
Who leads and who follows?	There is "one leader in the room"—the formal leader. Team members follow.	There is "leadership from every chair." At any point, any team member may lead and others may follow.
Who is accountable for how the team works together?	The formal leader.	Every team member.
Who are team members accountable to?	The formal leader.	Every team member.
Who or what determines the basis for effective team action?	The formal leader.	The team's guiding principles.
How are team structures and processes designed?	Congruent with unilateral control core values and assumptions.	Congruent with mutual learning core values and assumptions.
How are decisions made?	In a range of ways, but driven by a unilateral control mindset.	In a range of ways, but driven by a mutual learning mindset.

Don't fall back into the unilateral control pattern of trying to prepare an airtight case for the team to adopt the mutual learning approach. Be eager to welcome whatever reactions and insights the team has to offer. The point of this conversation is to reach agreement on understanding and experimenting with the approach.

DIGGING DEEPER

Once the team grasps the mutual learning and unilateral control approaches as well as the importance of team design, they should be able to start to discuss how they see the team in terms of these models. How do they see the team's current results? To what extent do they see the mutual learning and unilateral control approaches contributing to these results? Ideally, at the end of this conversation, you and your team will have some agreement about the need for change even if you're not yet deciding whether to adopt the mutual learning approach as a team.

Ask team members how they think the team is doing in the three types of results—performance, working relationships, and individual well-being. Add transparency to your curiosity by sharing your own views. By the end of this part of the conversation, you and the team should have reached some common understanding about the team's results. If people also see a gap between current results and expectations, move on to exploring the causes.

Where the team identifies results that haven't met expectations, ask them to trace those results back to team design, behaviors, and mindset. Start by asking team members to give specific examples showing how some team behaviors and team design elements led to these results. Then ask how team members' mindsets may have contributed to these behaviors and to aspects of current team design. When you finish, the team should have a causal story about how its mindset leads to design and behaviors that lead to specific results. Now get everyone curious. To what extent do they see the unilateral control approach hindering the team's results? If they see a significant contribution, then the team can move to discussing whether the mindset of mutual learning could provide the first rung in climbing back up through better behaviors and results.

After that you can also begin to jointly identify team structures, processes, and context elements that lead to weaker team results. For example, if your team is having challenges working with other teams in the organization, you might find that the boundary management roles need to be clearer. If your team takes a long time to make decisions or is regularly revisiting them, you might find that the process you use for problem solving and decision making needs to be reconsidered. As you think more about potential causes, you may also find that the team vision and mission aren't as clear or as well shared as they need to be. Because your team is a system, you will probably see multiple causes for any one result.

You and your team may find that members differ in the unilateral control behaviors they primarily use. Some may commonly state their views without asking genuine questions while others ask rhetorical questions without stating their views. Some may routinely focus on positions while others routinely make assumptions without testing them with others.

Remember that because your team is a system, team members will respond to one another's behaviors. As a result, you may find patterns in which one team member starts to state views without asking genuine questions, which leads to other team members doing the same, which leads the team to increasingly focus on positions and withhold relevant information, which ultimately leads to increased defensiveness and lower-quality decisions. By identifying the main patterns in the team, you can better understand how each team member affects team results.

Your team will probably need time to prepare for the tasks I've just described. You're asking them to reflect on team design, and on their own behavior and mindsets, as well as those of their fellow team members. If they have little experience with this type of conversation, they may want to think about it on their own and discuss it at later meetings. Rather than unilaterally planning to have or delay this next conversation, discuss the timing with the team and jointly plan when to talk.

JOINT PLANNING

Joint planning occurs at two points: At first when you and your team are discussing and deciding whether to learn about and experiment with the mutual learning approach, and later when you're working out whether and how to use the approach.

Regarding the first stage, in my more than thirty years of helping leadership teams learn about and apply the mutual learning approach, I've found that initially it takes a certain intensity of learning to experiment with shifting from unilateral control. It's not that the mutual learning approach is hard to understand. Conceptually, it's relatively simple. As my then twelve-year-old son, Noah, said to me when I gave him an article to read about the approach, "Dad, a lot of it seems like common sense." The hard part is turning common sense into common practice—consistently operating from a mutual learning mindset. To jump-start this learning and experimentation typically requires that you and your team spend a few days identifying how you get stuck and learning to shift to a mutual learning mindset. A consultant knowledgeable in mutual learning can help you.

If and when you reach the point at which team members understand the conceptual framework and agree to work toward change at the level of mindset, you'll want to agree on the specific results the team wants to achieve, compared with current results. You will also want to jointly redesign context, structures, and processes that should also change. Also agree to jointly design elements that will make sharing feedback throughout the team safer and more productive, along with other means of supporting everyone's progress.

Goals

Work on team goals can proceed in ways similar to your earlier individual work: the mutual learning goals that the team sets for itself should evolve directly from earlier conversations about the gaps between what the team needs to achieve and what it is currently achieving. For John Haley's leadership team, the immediate goal was to agree on a new business strategy. To accomplish that, they needed to set goals for asking genuine questions, testing assumptions, and discussing undiscussable issues. That meant becoming more curious and accountable.

Consider setting shorter-term goals as well. By doing so the team will more quickly determine how well it is moving toward achieving its longer-term goals. In addition to setting overall goals for performance, working relationships, and individual well-being, remember to set goals for specific meetings, conversations, e-mail exchanges, and decisions.

You'll also need to plan to measure progress toward the goals— it really is true that what gets counted counts. Measuring results increases the chance that people will focus on achieving them and making corrections when results fall short. You may already have measures in place. They don't have to be elaborate. In the case of Jay's team, the measure was simple. Did the team have a strategy that they were implementing? In another leadership team lead by a VP, one of the goals was for team members to solve business problems strategically without being inappropriately dependent on the leader. The VP kept a simple measure of how often people came to request solutions to problems they could solve on their own.

Support and Other Arrangements

One advantage of learning the mutual learning approach as a team is that team members can support each other in building mindset and skills. By giving each other feedback, your team members can increase the speed at which the team can achieve its goals. But to support each other, team members need to know one another's strengths and weaknesses regarding mutual learning. And that means that the team discusses this in the team. That is part of shared team leadership.

Team members will also want to reach agreement on when to work consciously at the approach. Obviously, if your team has decided to apply mutual learning it will use it in team meetings. But what about outside team meetings? Will individual team members use the approach when meeting with each other? When meeting with their respective teams? When meeting with others in the organization or outside it? The more you all practice it in different settings, the more rapidly your skills will accrue and the more authentic they will become.

There are various ways to design mutual learning into regular team meetings, before, beginning, during, and at the end. Before each meeting, share accountability by jointly planning the agenda. Team members can contribute items and the meeting chair—a role often rotated among team members—can take the lead in setting the order.

At the beginning of meetings, agree on the purpose and process for the meeting before diving into the agenda topics. See the discussion of Behavior 7 in Chapter Five to review this. Also agree on how the team will share responsibility for using mutual learning. In some leadership teams, although all the members are expected to use the whole approach, each member takes responsibility for tracking the use of one core value or behavior. Seeing that someone has missed an opportunity to use that core value or behavior, the responsible member intervenes to help bring it into play. Seeing that others have used a core value or behavior particularly well, the responsible member gives positive feedback. In other teams, everyone takes responsibility both for using the full approach and for giving feedback to others during the meeting.

During team meetings, if a significant team issue arises that was not on the agenda, either take time to explore it then or schedule time to explore it later. One powerful advantage of using the mutual learning approach is that team members raise important topics that were previously undiscussable. As a result, the team learns more about how it is working—and not working—and how it can better achieve its goals. In one team meeting, a member said he didn't see the need for team members to be interdependent with each other. This was a significant statement, since the organization's values included collaboration and the team leader believed that team members were interdependent. In a team without a mutual learning skill set and mindset, either the team member would not have raised the topic or, if he had, it would have been shut down by the team leader or others those who disagreed with him. In this case, the team quickly identified each member's views on the topic and agreed to schedule more time at a later meeting to discuss it in depth.

At the end of meetings, take a few minutes for members to review how they applied mutual learning well and what they will do differently next time. The more specific they can be in their review, the better the team will apply the learning.

BE CLEAR ABOUT THE DECISION-MAKING RULE

What do you do if you believe your team needs to use a mutual learning approach but some team members don't think it's necessary? Do you decide not to move forward? Do you have only those team members who see the value of mutual learning start to use it? Do you decide that the entire team will start using the approach anyway?

Leaders in different organizations handle this situation in different ways. Some leaders have set the explicit expectation that mutual learning is the way their team will do business and that everyone will learn and use it. One leader who expected everyone in the organization to do so made learning the approach a condition of employment. In some cases, leaders have removed direct reports from their team after coming to the conclusion that they weren't willing or able to use a mutual learning approach. In other cases, leaders decided to model the approach for the team and see if that changed team members' views. Other leaders have told their teams they want them to make an informed choice about whether to use a mutual learning approach. They required the team to learn the approach as a team and then decide whether it would be sufficiently valuable to use in the team.

One head of organization development told leaders the organization was making the mutual learning approach available for them to learn because it would help them lead more effectively, including developing strong working relationships—something the organization had been receiving complaints about. When several leaders publicly doubted that the organization would spend money without requiring the leaders to use the approach, the head of OD had an answer. She said that the organization was helping leaders learn the mutual learning approach because it was seen as valuable. Whether anyone used that approach or another approach was their choice. But, in any case, every leader would be held accountable not only for performance but also for developing and maintaining strong working relationships.

Underlying all these ways of making the decision is the same tension. How do you balance the team members' ability to make an informed choice with your ultimate accountability for the performance of the team? There's no one right answer. The mutual learning approach doesn't say that you have to let the team decide or that you have to decide, or anything in between. The mutual learning approach says that whatever decision-making rule you use—consensus, voting, you decide—the process leading up to the decision needs to use the mutual learning core values, assumptions, and behaviors. If you use the mutual learning mindset and skill set, then team members are likely to say that the process was fair, even if they disagree with the final decision.

Still, ideally you want your entire team to reach agreement on whether to learn and use the approach. To the extent that agreement is possible, the best way to create it is to use the mutual learning approach. Do team members differ over how well the team is doing? Over whether the unilateral control approach is a significant cause of team challenges? Over whether mutual learning will help the team get better results? Then get curious. Ask, "What needs do you have that wouldn't be met by using the approach?" "Is there any information you have that leads you to be concerned?" Help team members identify assumptions they are making that may lead them to conclude that the approach would not be helpful. One way to do this is to ask team members, "What conditions would you need in order for you to be willing to learn and try the approach?" About their responses, continue to be curious: "What about those conditions would make a difference?" Then jointly design a way to create those conditions, if possible.

Whatever decision-making rule you use to decide whether the team will learn and practice the mutual learning approach, it's essential that you tell the team and tell them early in the process. You might say: "I want us to make the decision by team consensus, but if we're not able to reach consensus, then I'll reserve the right to make the decision myself, and explain why I made the decision as I did."

If you plan to simply make the decision on your own after hearing the team discussion, say so to the team. If you are willing to put the issue to a vote, say that.

In any case, don't say at the outset that you've already decided that the team will be learning and using the approach. If that's what you're thinking, then saying it would be transparent. But then you've unilaterally taken a position and made a decision without hearing others' views because you're thinking that you understand the situation and they don't—and you're back in unilateral control.

BE THE CHANGE . . .

There is a paradox in talking with your team about the results it's getting and how unilateral control may contribute to those results. For team members to move toward mutual learning, they need to discuss how their using a unilateral control approach is hindering them. But to have a productive conversation about that requires mutual learning skills that team members—and perhaps you—don't yet have. In other words, this conversation is necessary, but it's also the kind of high-stakes conversation that requires a fair amount of mutual learning skills to generate good results.

One way to resolve this paradox is to ask a third party to guide the team to a productive conversation by helping them use the mutual learning approach during the meeting. This party might be another leader in your organization who has been using the mutual learning approach, a consultant inside your organization that knows it, or someone else from outside the organization.

As you talk with your team about changing, it's easy to fall into one of two unilateral control modes: either you tell the team only what you think and try to convince them, or you ask them leading questions that you hope will get them to realize that they are indeed unilaterally controlling and they do indeed need to move to mutual learning. Instead, try another approach: describe and be the change you want to see. Be as curious about team members' views as you are passionate about your own view.

Curiosity and compassion go hand-in-hand. It's easy to stop being curious when you lose your compassion. And it's easy to lose your compassion when you're feeling annoyed or impatient because team members don't seem to understand what you do, or because team members see things differently. If you start to feel this way, remind yourself that you're at a different point than they are. Along your way through this book, you've spent time reflecting on what the team can achieve and what it is currently achieving, and thought about the various causes of this gap. There were probably times when you read something that was hard to accept. At other points you simply disagreed. Still, if you've read this far, you're probably energized about the possibility of change and eager to start. You have done all this at your own pace, stopping to think when you needed more time. But you have made this journey alone, so your team is not in the same place.

Be compassionate about the ways in which this conversation can be challenging for your team. Some members may not have thought about the gap between the team's desired and current results or if they have, didn't see a large gap. Other members may see a gap but aren't sure that the change is worth the effort. With change comes concern. By being genuinely curious and compassionate about their concerns, you will be better able to jointly craft next steps with the team. At the same time, be transparent and accountable and hold your team members accountable, too. Where you and others have contributed to team challenges, say so, being specific and inviting reactions.

Together their corresponding assumptions, transparency, curiosity, informed choice, accountability, and compassion have the power to energize and transform you and your team. What at first may seem awkward and scary becomes natural and motivating in ways that you and your team may never have imagined. The results are improved performance, stronger working relationships, and greater well-being for you and your team.

Be compassionate about the ways in which this conversation can be challenging for your team.

Notes

Chapter 1

1. Argyris, C., and D. Schön (1974). *Increasing professional effectiveness: A theory of action perspective* (San Francisco: Jossey-Bass).
2. See Chris Argyris and Don Schön's work as well as Peter Block's 1993 book *Stewardship* (San Francisco: Berrett-Koehler).
3. Argyris and Schön (1974) described these two elements as theory-in-use and espoused theory.
4. Chris Argyris originally referred to this distinction as your espoused theory and theory-in-use.
5. This is not a new idea. In the early 1900s, the organizational theorist Mary Parker Follett described how a common purpose served as an invisible leader and created a partnership between leaders and followers that she called *reciprocal leadership*. Her work was published posthumously in *Dynamic administration: The collected papers of Mary Parker Follett,* edited by H. C. Metcalf and L. Urwick (New York: HarperCollins, 1941).
6. The unilateral control and mutual learning mindsets are derived from the 1978 work of Chris Argyris and Don Schön, who originally labeled them Model I and Model II, and from adaptations by Robert Putnam, Diana McLain Smith, and Phil MacArthur at Action Design (1997),

who use the terms I've chosen. See Argyris, C., and D. A. Schön (1978), *Organizational learning: A theory of action perspective* (Reading, MA: Addison-Wesley), and Putnam, R., D. M. Smith, et al., *Action Design: Workshop materials* (Newton, MA: Action Design, 1997).

Chapter 2

1. These core values originally were developed by Chris Argyris and Don Schön.
2. These assumptions and the mutual learning mindset assumptions were originally developed by Action Design. (See Smith, Putnam, et al., *Action Design.*)

Chapter 3

1. Mesmer-Magnus, J. R., and L. A. DeChurch (2009). "Information sharing and team performance: A meta-analysis." *Journal of Applied Psychology* 94(2): 535–546.
2. Wanberg, C. R., and J. T. Banas (2000). "Predictors and outcomes of openness to changes in a reorganizing workplace." *Journal of Applied Psychology* 85(1): 132–142.
3. Jassawalla, A. R., H. C. Sashittal, et al. (2010). "Effects of transparency and at-stakeness on students' perceptions of their ability to work collaboratively in effective classroom teams: A partial test of the Jassawalla and Sashittal Model." *Decision Sciences Journal of Innovative Education* 8(1): 35–53.
4. Edmondson, A. C. (2003). "Speaking up in the operating room: How team leaders promote learning in interdisciplinary action teams." *Journal of Management Studies* 40(6): 1419–1452.
5. Tschan, F., N. K. Semmer, et al. (2009). "Explicit reasoning, confirmation bias, and illusory transactive memory: A simulation study of group medical decision making." *Small Group Research* 40(3): 271–300.
6. Moye, N. A., and C. W. Langfred (2004). "Information sharing and group conflict: Going beyond decision making to understand the effects of information sharing on group performance." *International Journal of Conflict Management* 15(4): 381–410.
7. Sack, K. (May 18, 2008). "Doctors say 'I'm sorry' before 'see you in court.'" *New York Times.*
8. Kouzes, J. M., and B. Z. Posner (1993). *Credibility: How leaders gain and lose it, why people demand it* (San Francisco: Jossey-Bass). Quotes on pp. 12, 48, 51.

9. Bennis, W. G., D. Goleman, et al. (2008). *Transparency: How leaders create a culture of candor* (San Francisco: Jossey-Bass). Quote on pp. 61–62.

10. Norman, S. M., B. J. Avolio, et al. (2010). "The impact of positivity and transparency on trust in leaders and their perceived effectiveness." *Leadership Quarterly* 21(3): 350–364.

11. Re motivation: Kay, B., and D. M. Christophel (1995). "The relationships among manager communication openness, nonverbal immediacy, and subordinate motivation." *Communication Research Reports* 12(2): 200–205. Re job satisfaction: Burke, R. J., and D. S. Wilcox (1969). "Effects of different patterns and degrees of openness in superior-subordinate communication on subordinate job satisfaction." *Academy of Management Journal* 12(3): 319–326. See also Korsgaard, M. A., S. E. Brodt, et al. (2002). "Trust in the face of conflict: The role of managerial trustworthy behavior and organizational context." *Journal of Applied Psychology* 87(2): 312–319.

12. Schilpzand, M. C., D. M. Herold, et al. (2011). "Members' openness to experience and teams' creative performance." *Small Group Research* 42(1): 55–76. See also Homan, A. C., J. R. Hollenbeck, et al. (2008). "Facing differences with an open mind: Openness to experience, salience of intragroup differences, and performance of diverse work groups." *Academy of Management Journal* 51(6): 1204–1222.

13. Nair, K. U., and S. Ramnarayan (2000). "Individual differences in need for cognition and complex problem solving." *Journal of Research in Personality* 34(3): 305–328.

14. Reio, T. G., Jr., and A. Wiswell (2000). "Field investigation of the relationship among adult curiosity, workplace learning, and job performance." *Human Resource Development Quarterly* 11(1): 5–30.

15. LePine, J. A. (2003). "Team adaptation and postchange performance: Effects of team composition in terms of members' cognitive ability and personality." *Journal of Applied Psychology* 88(1): 27–39.

16. Cacioppo, J. T., R. E. Petty, et al. (1996). "Dispositional differences in cognitive motivation: The life and times of individuals varying in need for cognition." *Psychological Bulletin* 119(2): 197–253.

17. Homan, Hollenbeck, et al. "Facing differences with an open mind."

18. Kashdan, T. (2009). *Curious? Discover the missing ingredient to a fulfilling life* (New York: Collins Living). Discussion pp. 35–50.

19. Kashdan, *Curious?* p. 137.

20. Matsumoto, D., J. LeRoux, et al. (2000). "A new test to measure emotion recognition ability: Matsumoto and Ekman's Japanese and Caucasian

Brief Affect Recognition Test (JACBART)." *Journal of Nonverbal Behavior* 24(3): 179–209.

21. Kashdan, *Curious?* Discussion on pp. 35–50.

22. Fairfield, K. D., and K. G. Allred (2007). "Skillful inquiry as a means to success in mixed-motive negotiation." *Journal of Applied Social Psychology* 37(8): 1837–1855.

23. Gallagher, M. W., and S. J. Lopez (2007). "Curiosity and well-being." *Journal of Positive Psychology* 2: 236–248; Kashdan, T. B., and M. F. Steger (2007). "Curiosity and pathways to well-being and meaning in life: Traits, states, and everyday behaviors." *Motivation and Emotion* 31: 159–173.

24. Fairfield and Allred, "Skillful inquiry as a means to success in mixed-motive negotiation."

25. Kashdan and Steger, "Curiosity and pathways to well-being and meaning in life."

26. Losada, M. (1999). "The complex dynamics of high performance teams." *Mathematical and Computer Modelling* 30(9–10): 179–192.

27. Wood, J. A., Jr., and B. E. Winston (2005). "Toward a new understanding of leader accountability: Defining a critical construct." *Journal of Leadership & Organizational Studies* 11(3): 84–94.

28. Carmeli, A., Z. Sheaffer, et al. (2009). "Does participatory decision-making in top management teams enhance decision effectiveness and firm performance?" *Personnel Review* 38(6): 696–714.

29. Carmeli, A. (2008). "Top management team behavioral integration and the performance of service organizations." *Group & Organization Management* 33(6): 712–735.

30. Black, J. S., and H. B. Gregersen (1997). "Participative decision-making: An integration of multiple dimensions." *Human Relations* 50(7): 859–878.

31. Scott-Ladd, B., A. Travaglione, et al. (2006). "Causal inferences between participation in decision making, task attributes, work effort, rewards, job satisfaction and commitment." *Leadership & Organization Development Journal* 27(5): 399–414.

32. Kashdan, *Curious?*

33. Carmeli, "Top management team behavioral integration. . . ."

34. Scott-Ladd, Travaglione, et al. "Causal inferences. . . ."

35. Black and Gregersen, "Particpative decision-making."

36. Davis, W. D., N. Mero, et al. (2007). "The interactive effects of goal orientation and accountability on task performance." *Human Performance* 20(1): 1–21.

37. Ford, J. K., and E. Weldon (1981). "Forewarning and accountability: Effects on memory-based interpersonal judgments." *Personality and Social Psychology Bulletin* 7(2): 264–268. Siegel-Jacobs, K., and J. F. Yates (1996). "Effects of procedural and outcome accountability on judgment quality." *Organizational Behavior & Human Decision Processes* 65(1): 1–17.

38. Ashton, R. H. (1992). "Effects of justification and a mechanical aid on judgment performance." *Organizational Behavior & Human Decision Processes* 52(2): 292–306. Mero, N. P., and S. J. Motowidlo (1995). "Effects of rater accountability on the accuracy and the favorability of performance ratings." *Journal of Applied Psychology* 80(4): 517–524. Brtek, M. D., and S. J. Motowidlo (2002). "Effects of procedure and outcome accountability on interview validity." *Journal of Applied Psychology* 87(1): 185–191.

39. Scholten, L., D. van Knippenberg, et al. (2007). "Motivated information processing and group decision-making: Effects of process accountability on information processing and decision quality." *Journal of Experimental Social Psychology* 43(4): 539–552.

40. Rozelle, R. M., and J. C. Baxter (1981). "Influence of role pressures on the perceiver: Judgments of videotape interviews varying judge accountability and responsibility." *Journal of Applied Psychology* 66(4): 437–441.

41. Tetlock, P. E. (1985). "Accountability: A social check on the fundamental attribution error." *Social Psychology Quarterly* 48(3): 227–236.

42. Jordan, P., and A. C. Troth (2004). "Managing emotions during team problem solving." *Human Performance* 17(2): 195–218. Rosete, D., and J. Ciarrochi (2005). "Emotional intelligence and its relationship to workplace performance outcomes of leadership effectiveness." *Leadership & Organization Development Journal* 26(5): 388–399.

43. Allred, K. G., J. S. Mallozzi, et al. (1997). "The influence of anger and compassion on negotiation performance." *Organizational Behavior & Human Decision Processes* 70(3): 175–187.

44. Condon, P., and D. DeSteno (2011). "Compassion for one reduces punishment for another." *Journal of Experimental Social Psychology* 47(3): 698–701. Rudolph, U., S. C. Roesch, et al. (2004). "A meta-analytic review of help giving and aggression from an attributional perspective: Contributions to a general theory of motivation." *Cognition & Emotion* 18(6): 815–848.

45. Grant, A. M., J. E. Dutton, et al. (2008). "Giving commitment: Employee support programs and the prosocial sensemaking process." *Academy of Management Journal* 51(5): 898–918.

46. Berke, D. (1995). *The Gentle Smile* (New York: Crossroad Publishing).
47. Quote available online: www.gandhitopia.org/forum/topics/a-gandhi -quote?xg_source=activity; access date: September 24, 2012.
48. Edmondson, A. (1999). "Psychological safety and learning behavior in work teams." *Administrative Science Quarterly* 44(2): 350–383.
49. Stata, R. (1989). "Organizational learning—the key to management innovation." *Sloan Management Review* 30(3): 63–74.
50. Edmondson, "Psychological safety and learning behavior in work teams."
51. Oldham, G. R., and J. R. Hackman (1980). "Work design in the organizational context." *Research in Organizational Behavior* 2: 247.

Chapter 5

1. Mary Parker Follett first discussed the idea of focusing on and integrating interests to solve conflicts in her 1925 paper "Constructive Conflict" (see *Dynamic administration: The collected papers of Mary Parker Follett*, edited by H. C. Metcalf and L. Urwick [New York: HarperCollins, 1941]). The concept was popularized and the phrase "focus on interests, not positions" comes from Fisher, R., W. Ury, et al. (1991). *Getting to yes: Negotiating agreement without giving in*, 2nd ed. (NY: Penguin).
2. I have adapted this story from one that originally appeared in Mary Parker Follett's 1925 paper "Constructive Conflict" (see *Dynamic administration*). It also appears in Fisher, Ury, et al. *Getting to yes*.
3. Chris Argyris introduced the ladder of inference in *Reasoning, learning, and action: Individual and organizational* (San Francisco: Jossey-Bass, 1982). Drawing on Argyris's work, Peter Senge popularized it in *The Fifth Discipline: The Art and Practice of the Learning Organization* (New York: Doubleday, 1992, 1993). John Dewey discussed the inferential process in his work in the early 1900s; see Dewey, J. (1910). *How We Think* (Lexington, MA: Heath).
4. Ryan, K. D., and D. K. Oestreich (1991). *Driving fear out of the workplace: How to overcome the invisible barriers to quality, productivity, and innovation* (San Francisco: Jossey-Bass).
5. Ryan and Oestreich, *Driving fear out of the workplace*. Forty-four percent of people interviewed in this study cited fear of repercussions for not speaking up.

Chapter 6

1. Allport, F. H. (1967). "A theory of enestruence (event-structure theory): Report of progress." *American Psychologist* 22(1): 1–24.

2. Hackman, R. J. (2002). *Leading teams: Setting the stage for great performances* (Boston: Harvard Business Press).

3. Hackman, *Leading teams.*

4. Locke, E. A., and G. P. Latham (2002). "Building a practically useful theory of goal setting and task motivation." *American Psychologist* 57(9): 705–716.

5. Hackman, J. R. (1987). "The design of work teams." In J. Lorsch (ed.), *Handbook of organizational behavior* (Upper Saddle River, NJ: Prentice-Hall).

6. Karau, S. J., and K. D. Williams (1993). "Social loafing: A meta-analytic review and theoretical integration." *Journal of Personality and Social Psychology* 65(4): 681–706.

7. Argyris, C., and D. A. Schön (1978). *Organizational learning: A theory of action perspective* (Reading, MA: Addison-Wesley).

8. Schein, E. H. (1985). *Organizational culture and leadership* (San Francisco: Jossey-Bass). See also Argyris, C. (1990). *Overcoming organizational defenses: Facilitating organizational learning* (Boston: Allyn & Bacon).

9. Schein, E. H. (1987). *Process consultation: Lessons for managers and consultants,* Vol. 2 (Reading, MA: Addison-Wesley).

10. Mccrae, R. R. (1996). "Social consequences of experiential openness." *Psychological Bulletin* 120: 323–337.

11. Amason, A. C. (1996). "Distinguishing the effects of functional and dysfunctional conflict on strategic decision making: Resolving a paradox for top management teams." *Academy of Management Journal* 39(1): 123–148.

12. Sundstrom, E., K. P. DeMeuse, et al. (1990). "Work teams: Applications and effectiveness." *American Psychologist* 45(2), 120–133.

13. Kerr, S. (1975). On the folly of rewarding A, while hoping for B. *Academy of Management Journal* 18: 769–783.

14. Carlson, P. (2005). "Do surveys provide valid information for organizational change?" In R. Schwarz, A. Davidson, P. Carlson, and S. McKinney (eds.), *The skilled facilitator fieldbook: Tips, tools, and tested methods for consultants, facilitators, managers, trainers, and coaches,* pp. 409–412 (San Francisco: Jossey-Bass).

Chapter 7

1. Many of the topics in this chapter were originally published in my monthly idea letter, "Mindset. Behavior. Results."

Chapter 8

1. Edmondson, A. (1999). Psychological safety and learning behavior in work teams. *Administrative Science Quarterly* 44: 350–383.

Acknowledgments

Many people helped me bring this book to fruition and I want to thank them. My clients over the years have shared their concerns with me, trusted me to help them create significant change, and helped me hone the approach that you see in these pages.

My colleagues Dan Denison and Diana McLain Smith gave me valuable feedback on an initial draft of this book, which helped me refine the structure. Adam Grant, who has an encyclopedic—should I say Wikipedic?—knowledge of the field, pointed me to relevant research that I wasn't aware of. Ed Lawler, Stew Friedman, and Dan Denison helped me think about how to bring the book to the attention of leaders. The research and writing of Chris Argyris and Don Schön and Richard Hackman provided solid foundations that I have used in this book—and in Roger Schwarz & Associates (RSA) work in general. The work of my colleagues at Action Design—Diana McLain Smith, Bob Putnam, and Phil MacArthur—has also influenced my work.

My colleagues at RSA helped me in many ways. For more than twenty years, Anne Davidson has been my primary partner in helping leaders and teams create better results with a mutual learning approach. Many of the ideas in this book are the result of conversations that Anne and I have had as we've traveled together to work with clients. Peg Carlson has played a similar role. Both have helped me think through what makes for mutual learning leaders and teams and how best to work with our clients to achieve their results. Anne and Betty Johnson read through each chapter— sometimes more than once. Anne identified places where I didn't clearly state what I meant and where I was giving advice that might be misinterpreted. Betty made sure that I was always focused on you the reader in a way that best served your needs. Peg and Carrie Hays also gave me feedback on chapters. My sister Dale Schwarz helped me think through the role of compassion in mutual learning. In addition, she has supported me throughout my writing the book (as well as my entire life). Mike Mitchell helped me with all sorts of computer problems so I could maintain my productivity. Lois Kurtz handled administrative matters as the book entered production.

Kathe Sweeney, my editor at Jossey-Bass, is a joy to work with. She believes deeply in the mutual learning approach and convinced me to write this book for a broader audience—leaders of leadership teams. She participated in RSA's workshop on mutual learning, spent three days with me in Boston structuring and restructuring the book, and gave me constant support with patience even as I delayed the book schedule.

Alan Venable, my development editor, took a first draft and helped shaped it into a structure that made it easier and more compelling for readers. His feedback—negative and positive—was clear, concise, and compassionate. Mary Garrett, my production editor, efficiently guided me and the project in the final phase, producing the book you now hold in your hands. Hilary Powers, my copyeditor, tightened my writing while maintaining my voice—and modeled mutual learning when she gave me feedback. Adrian Morgan designed the book cover, responding quickly to our needs.

David Kerr, our design consultant, created graphics of the models in the book.

Carolyn Monaco and Alicia Simons at Monaco Associates, working closely with Betty Johnson, have advised, managed, and helped execute our plan for bringing the book to the attention of readers. After all, if a book hits the market and no one reads it, does it make an impact?

Finally, I want to thank my spouse, Kathleen, and our children, Noah and Hannah. They have been wonderfully supportive of my writing this book. Over the years, Noah and Hannah have developed their mutual learning mindset and skill set. They continue to become more transparent and curious, holding themselves and others accountable, all while becoming more compassionate. It has constantly enriched our relationships. Kathleen has been a natural model for me of curiosity and compassion. She has helped me become a better spouse, father, and overall human being. This book is dedicated to the three of them.

About the Author

Roger Schwarz, a recognized thought leader in team leadership and improving team effectiveness, is a sought-after adviser to global companies, federal government agencies, and nonprofit organizations. He is the author of the bestselling *The Skilled Facilitator*, and is president and CEO of Roger Schwarz & Associates.

Through his work and writing, Roger's mission is to help create teams and organizations that are innovative and successful, and that honor the best of who we are as human beings. He accomplishes this by enabling leaders to change the way they think and work so that they can raise and resolve the tough issues, working with their teams to get unstuck and get better results.

For more than thirty years, Roger has consulted, taught, facilitated, coached, and spoken with groups on how to create more effective leadership teams. Prior to founding Roger Schwarz & Associates, he served as tenured associate professor of public management and government and assistant director at the Institute of Government at the University of North Carolina at Chapel Hill. He earned his BS degree in psychology from Tufts University, AM and PhD in organizational psychology from the University of Michigan, and his MEd degree from Harvard University.

Roger lives in Chapel Hill, North Carolina, where he uses mutual learning with his wife and community, and with his two young adult children who periodically come home to visit.

Index

About Roger Schwarz & Associates

Roger Schwarz & Associates, Inc., provides a rigorous and compassionate method for leaders and leadership teams to get unstuck, get more done, and hit their goals. Through diagnosis, consulting, training, facilitation, coaching, and measurements, leaders and their teams at the Boeing Company, the World Bank, the U.S. Department of the Interior, Chevron, Lockheed Martin, and other world-class organizations have resolved their toughest challenges to create significantly better results.

To learn more about how Roger Schwarz & Associates can help your leadership team be more effective, visit www.schwarzassociates .com.

INTRODUCING THE SMART LEADERS, SMARTER TEAMS KEYNOTE

When stakes are high, you and your team can't get great results by just changing what you do. You also need to change how you think. Organizational psychologist and leadership consultant Roger Schwarz applies his more than thirty years' experience working with leadership teams to reveal how leaders can dramatically improve results by changing their individual and team mindset. In his keynote, Roger

- Provides practical ways leaders can improve decision quality, reduce costs, and get greater commitment
- Provides a clear contrast to the less effective approach most leaders and leadership teams operate from
- Outlines five core values leadership teams can adopt today to significantly improve results

To learn more about Roger's speaking, contact him at: contactroger@schwarzassociates.com.

MORE ABOUT ROGER SCHWARZ & ASSOCIATES' WORK WITH CLIENTS

Roger Schwarz & Associates delivers a rigorous and compassionate method for leaders and leadership teams to get to the heart of their toughest challenges and realize their greatest opportunities.

Get started:

- Attend an open-enrollment workshop.
- Book a one-day overview to introduce Smart Leaders, Smarter Teams to your team.
- Engage a team facilitator to work with your team on your real work.

Change the way you think and how you work. Your team will get unstuck, get more done, and hit your goals.

Learn more at: www.schwarzassociates.com.